SUPER HUSBAND,
SUPER DAD

You Can Be the Hero Your Family Needs

Tim Shoemaker

HARVEST HOUSE PUBLISHERS
EUGENE, OREGON

Unless otherwise indicated, all Scripture quotations are taken from the Holy Bible, New International Version®, NIV®. Copyright © 1973, 1978, 1984, 2011 by Biblica, Inc.® Used by permission. All rights reserved worldwide.

Verses marked (NLT) are taken from the Holy Bible, New Living Translation, copyright © 1996, 2004, 2007 by Tyndale House Foundation. Used by permission of Tyndale House Publishers, Inc., Carol Stream, Illinois 60188. All rights reserved.

Cover by Aesthetic Soup, Shakopee, Minnesota

Cover photo © iStock / Remains

Published in association with Hartline Literary Agency, LLC, of 123 Queenston Drive, Pittsburgh, PA 15235.

SUPER HUSBAND, SUPER DAD

Copyright © 2014 Tim Shoemaker
Published by Harvest House Publishers
Eugene, Oregon 97402
www.harvesthousepublishers.com

Library of Congress Cataloging-in-Publication Data
    Shoemaker, Tim.
    Super husband, super dad / Tim Shoemaker.
        pages cm
    ISBN 978-0-7369-5350-4 (pbk.)
    ISBN 978-0-7369-5351-1 (eBook)
    1. Husbands—Religious life. 2. Fathers—Religious life. 3. Fatherhood—Religious aspects—Christianity. I. Title.
    BV4528.3.S56 2014
    248.8'421—dc23

                                                            2013043568

All rights reserved. No part of this publication may be reproduced, stored in a retrieval system, or transmitted in any form or by any means—electronic, mechanical, digital, photocopy, recording, or any other—except for brief quotations in printed reviews, without the prior permission of the publisher.

Printed in the United States of America

        14 15 16 17 18 19 20 21 22 / VP-JH / 10 9 8 7 6 5 4 3 2 1

To my three sons, Andy, Mark, and Luke.
May marriage and parenting bring you
every bit as much joy as it has me.

"I have no greater joy than to hear
that my children are walking in the truth."

3 John 4

And dedicated to you, the man reading this book,
and to the plans God has for you.

"Unless the LORD builds the house,
the builders labor in vain."

PSALM 127:1

Special thanks to...

Cec Murphy...for planting the first seed that I should write this book.

Kathleen Kerr...for convincing me to write this, for championing the manuscript, and for expert editing.

Noah Kerr...for a reaction to the manuscript that helped convince Kathleen it needed to be published.

My dad...for perfectly modeling so many of these principles to me.

My wife, Cheryl...I definitely wouldn't be here without you, Babe!

Contents

Introduction

Once upon a time, men wore the pants, and wore them well. Women rarely had to open doors and little old ladies never crossed the street alone. Men took charge because that's what they did. But somewhere along the way, the world decided it no longer needed men. Disco by disco, latte by non-fat latte, men were stripped of their khakis and left stranded on the road between boyhood and androgyny. But today there are questions our genderless society has no answers for. The world sits idly by as cities crumble, children misbehave and those little old ladies remain on one side of the street. For the first time since bad guys, we need heroes. We need grown-ups. We need men to put down the plastic fork, step away from the salad bar, and untie the world from the tracks of complacency. It's time to get your hands dirty. It's time to answer the call of manhood. It's time to wear the pants.

—FROM AN ADVERTISEMENT FOR DOCKERS JEANS

The first time I read this Levi's ad, I actually laughed. I liked it. Really liked it. Not surprisingly, the ad got some people riled up and was labeled as controversial.

But I think there is an element of truth here. I'm not suggesting that men need to get all Neanderthal and start treating women like objects or like they're inferior. Just the opposite. I think we're living in an age when men need to stand up and be men. To do the right thing even when it's hard. To exercise self-control. To love and lead their spouse and family well. In short, we need men to be heroes.

And that's what we're going to look at in this book. How to be the hero your family needs. Like the Levi's ad, there will likely be some things written in here that will be controversial. Some things might get you a little ticked off at me. Other things will cause you to suck in your breath and pause…and wonder what life might be like if you took the advice printed in these pages.

As men we need to step things up. Make changes if we expect to be the men, the husbands, and the dads God designed us to be. In every chapter I'm going to encourage you to be the hero your family needs. We'll talk about taking your role as a man to a higher level. Shifting into a higher gear. We'll talk about fighting the enemies of our soul, our marriage, and our family…and winning.

It's time to strap on your cape and be a hero. You can do this. We'll do it together.

You ready? Let's go fight some bad guys.

Burning Love

Cheryl and I were newlyweds when we signed up for a small weekend marriage conference. It sounded like a good idea...*until* I saw the speaker. White-haired and overweight, I couldn't imagine him bringing anything incredibly relevant to the table. I know, I know. That wasn't much of an attitude on my part.

But I had him pegged wrong. Totally. He said something that turned out to be the best parenting advice I ever got. Here it is: "If you want to be a good dad, love your wife." Then he addressed the women. "And if you want to be a good mom, love your husband."

You were expecting something more profound? You're ready to breeze by this and see what the next point is? Hold on for a moment. You're seeing the white hair and the big gut.

Here's the truth. I applied that old preacher's bit of advice, and over thirty years later I can testify that what he said was critically important. And it worked. I have an excellent marriage. My wife and I raised three adventure-loving boys together. None of them rebelled against God or us in their teens and we still enjoy an excellent relationship with them. The trickle-down effect of that pastor's wisdom is enormous.

> If you want to be a good dad, love your wife.

God in his grace gave me truth years ago, and he gave me the heart to believe and follow it. He nudged me back on track countless times. And now I believe I'm meant to pass it on to you.

Recently I had a problem with a couple of tires on my car. At certain speeds the car vibrated and the tires made a *whop, whop, whop, whop* noise. It was distracting and annoying. A tire dealer showed me how the tires had worn in an uneven, choppy pattern. They were getting to the point of being dangerous, so I replaced them.

Now, the real issue? Thanks to Chicago winters and resulting potholes, the alignment on my car was off—which eventually damaged the tires. I needed more than new tires for a smooth ride. I needed a realignment first. They go hand in hand.

It's the same with marriage and parenting. They're connected. If my marriage is out of alignment with the principles of God's Word, it will affect everything—kids and parenting included. If my marriage is adjusted right, let me tell you, the whole marriage and parenting ride is a *lot* smoother.

If you work on your marriage, your kids will be more secure. When Mom and Dad argue or are cold to each other...*that* breeds insecurity. Insecure kids react in a variety of ways, none of them good. Some go quiet. Some turn life into a circus, craving the attention in the center ring. Some act up in school. As they get older, some seek security from others—and many get taken advantage of as a result. Boys follow the wrong boys, and girls open themselves up to the wrong boys too—often because Mom and Dad didn't provide a secure atmosphere at home.

My car needed a realignment—and it damaged the tires because I didn't catch it in time. In a similar way, when a marriage is out of whack, it will show up in the kids eventually. As a parent, you want to do a great job raising your kids, right? You want them to be balanced. Strong. Able to stand on their own two feet. But know this. Unless you give your marriage as much and more attention than you do to raising the kids, you might as well run over your kids' toes with the car.

Because if you don't work on your marriage, you'll cripple your kids in a variety of ways.

So, for starters, take that advice I got years ago to heart, and add the principle we just talked about.

> If you want to be a good parent, love your mate. If your marriage is out of whack, it will show up in the kids eventually—and you're all in for a bumpy ride.

There's more to love than Hollywood...

Loving your mate isn't the type of thing you see in movies or read about in fiction. I know what you're thinking. *Of course. That kind of love isn't real. Real love isn't quite that passionate.* Hollywood love isn't real—you got that right. But real love isn't *less* than what you see in movies. It's more.

What does it take to love your mate? Chances are you're totally familiar with how 1 Corinthians 13 describes real love. Maybe your wife even has a cute plaque hanging in your home with the verses written in some fancy script. But if we're going to get this "love" thing right, we need to cover those verses. They represent the starting point for love in marriage. *Starting point.* Did you catch that?

First Corinthians is foundational for marital love, but it was never intended to give the whole picture. Surprised? Wait until you see what God's picture of love really is. But I'm getting ahead of myself. First, read 1 Corinthians 13:4-8.

> Love is patient, love is kind. It does not envy, it does not boast, it is not proud. It does not dishonor others, it is not self-seeking, it is not easily angered, it keeps no record of wrongs. Love does not delight in evil but rejoices with the truth. It always protects, always trusts, always hopes, always perseveres. Love never fails.

Great stuff. Classic. Total truth. And a road map for real love. We'll touch on a number of these principles as we go along in this book. But many people miss something critical in this passage—something about the context. First Corinthians was a letter written to the church. A group of believers. Chapter 12 talks about spiritual gifts. Gifts and abilities given to people in the church for the benefit of the *church body*. Love is one of those gifts. This passage describes the type of love we should give to *all Christians*—not just our mate. This describes committed, consistent, and self-sacrificing love. It is part of our Christian duty to give this kind of love.

★ ★ ★

Real love isn't *less* than what you see in movies. It's more.

★ ★ ★

But the love I show my mate should be something more than what I show others, right? Bingo. And the Bible *does* give us a picture of married love. First Corinthians 13 is foundational for what married love should be about, but there's also to be something more. Something we don't see in verses 4 through 8. What is it?

Passion.

First Corinthians doesn't fully describe the passion a man and wife should have for each other. It doesn't fully address the passion your marriage needs to keep it fresh. Strong. Excellent. Check out these verses from Song of Songs:

> Love is as strong as death, its jealousy unyielding as the grave. It burns like blazing fire, like a mighty flame. Many waters cannot quench love; rivers cannot sweep it away. If one were to give all the wealth of one's house for love, it would be utterly scorned (Song of Songs 8:6-7).

That is passion!

Love is as strong as death. Death conquers all, right? And so does love. It's the "love never fails" principle from 1 Corinthians 13, but with the passion of marriage behind it.

It burns like blazing fire. We're talking about a consuming fire here. It burns past all obstacles.

Many waters cannot quench love. This flame of love can't be doused. It goes back to the 1 Corinthians love that "always perseveres," but in marriage, it's more than mere duty. Passionate, unquenchable love is the goal...and the reward.

In fact, the passage goes on to say that giving up all you had for such love would not be some noble sacrifice. It would be totally worth it—because love is so valuable. In light of this, Hollywood love is a bit shallow.

Now, there was a time when your love for your mate had this intensity. But has it relaxed a bit? Gotten flabby? Or has this passionate love been focused someplace else? Often couples still have this passionate, unquenchable love, but not for their mate. It has been slowly redirected to the kids.

There's nothing wrong with passionately loving your kids. That's the way it should be. But if that replaces or eclipses the passionate love you have for your mate, you've got things upside down. You need a realignment.

Think about it. Your toddler son makes a mess of his dinner—and you take pictures to remember the moment. Your wife messes up on dinner—and you feel cheated.

Wives do it too. They'll coo over their baby and shower them with TLC and kisses during a diaper change. You want your wife to take your pants down and do a little of the same, and she's suddenly feeling taken advantage of. Unappreciated.

Hard truth...but truth. We need to get the raging fire, rushing waters, stronger-than-death kind of passion back in our love for our wife. A passionate marriage is the best way to help your kids, too—because a great marriage and great parenting go hand in hand. Hard to do one without the other.

So let's get a realignment. Bring our marriage back to the manufacturer's specs. Let's strengthen your marriage and get the passion going again—which is what this entire book is really about.

* * *

An Extra Ration of Passion

When you lose something like your car keys, the best way to find them is to go backward. Retrace your steps. You figure out the last place you *knew* you had your keys and then try to remember every little thing you did after that. Chances are, you'll find your keys. Going backward is often the best way to move forward.

But if you've lost the passion in your marriage, how do you find it again?

Revelation 2:4-5 is a message to the church in Ephesus, but it holds a clue to regaining passion in marriage as well. The church was going through the motions and doing a lot of things right, but the passion was gone. They are told to do two things.

Repent.

Do the things you did at first.

We can do the same in our marriage.

If our marriage has drifted into a state of mediocrity, we need to repent. That involves confession and a deliberate change of direction. Confess it to God. Ask for his help. And you may need to confess it to your wife, too.

Now, the change of direction. Think back to the days you and your wife dated and were first married. When your passion burned strong and hot for each other. When nothing could separate you from each other. When you hated to be apart and longed to be together. Think about the way you acted—the way you treated her back them. Remember the efforts you made for her in those early years of being together. What sacrifices and changes did you make? How hard did you work to please her—to make her happy?

17

It worked before, and it will again…if you dedicate yourself to it. Your marriage will get stronger, and you'll do something really good for the kids at the same time. You'll give them a secure home filled with love, and you'll etch an example in their mind of what a solid Christian marriage looks like. And it isn't just for the kids. A great marriage is a whole lot more fun.

The two of you have a history together. Go back and review it. Do the things you used to do. Repeat a little history—and watch how it changes your future.

Yes and No

One of the first words most kids learn is *no*. And as husbands, we probably still use that word far more often than we should. And sometimes we get that turned around. Upside down. We say *no* to our wives and *yes* to our kids when it should be the other way around.

Loving your mate has a lot to do with saying "yes" as often as you can.

"Honey, do think you could do me a favor?" *Yes.*

"Can you can give me an extra hand with the kids?" *Yes.*

You probably say *no* a lot more often than you think you do. Maybe your wife needs you to take on some project you've back-burnered. Maybe it has to do with attending events and functions on her side of the family. I know guys who always seem to come up with an excuse not to go with their wives to family functions. That, my friend, is a mistake. Huge. If you don't attend, family members may lose respect for you. It looks cowardly or selfish. And it'll be an embarrassment for your wife. Do you want that? You should want to be with her—*no matter where she goes.* Protect your marriage, bro. Say yes, and make the time fun. Don't be a martyr about it. That isn't manly.

Sometimes a wife wants her husband to take her out or to do something she thinks is fun. Be quick to say *yes* to that. Sometimes a woman needs a bit more variety. A change of pace. A wise husband will help in these areas.

Want a stronger marriage? Say *yes* when your mate asks for your help in some way. And avoid saying *no* when your wife needs to be held. And I'm not just talking about the word *no*. I'm talking about body language, too. A guy who comes home from work growling about how tired he is and how he just wants to prop up his feet and handle the remote has already said no to any number of things his wife might want to ask him. Not smart.

What might happen if you said to your wife, "I've got thirty minutes and I'm all yours. What would you like me to do? If I can do it in thirty minutes, my answer is *yes*."

Saying "yes" to each other will make a difference in your marriage. And if you must say "no," come up with **creative alternatives**.

Remember playing "Mother May I" with friends as a kid? One kid plays "Mother" while the rest line up facing her on the opposite side of the yard. The object was to be the first one to tag "Mother"—but you had to get permission, of sorts, to move forward before you could do it.

"Mother, may I take three giant steps forward?"

"No, you may not," Mother would say. "But you may take one baby step and one scissors-step forward."

And so the game went. "Mother" came up with creative alternatives to let you advance in some way. If the person playing "Mother" did nothing but say no to every request to move forward, the whole thing would get really boring. We're talking game over.

And that is the point with creative alternatives. When you're talking to your wife and you have to say no for whatever reason, don't leave it there. Be sure to come up with a creative alternative.

Let's imagine she just needs you to listen to her, so she approaches you something like this.

"Honey, I need to talk to you about something."

Imagine you're totally tied up at the moment. Honestly? Your best bet is to stop what you're doing and see what's up. But if you really can't drop what you're doing, explain it to your wife nicely and tell her when you *can* talk.

"Can you give me thirty minutes to tie this up? I want to give you my full attention, and I know my mind is going to keep running back to this if I don't finish it first." Say it in a way that makes it clear you *want* to talk to her—not like you are making some heroic sacrifice to do it. Get over yourself and remember this is part of your job and part of your calling. It is also an honor. A privilege. And remember, there are worse things than your wife wanting to talk to you.

Then watch the clock—because she will. If your thirty minutes turns into an hour you'd better wear a jacket. You won't be getting a warm reception. Be there in thirty minutes or less. Turn off your cell and give her your attention.

Think this is too hard to do? You're a *man*. Men do hard things without complaining. Use this time as a way to demonstrate love.

Work on that this week. *Tonight*. Make it a game. *Don't say no*.

★ ★ ★

If you must say *no*, come up with creative alternatives.

★ ★ ★

Loving your kids has a lot to do with saying yes and no at the right times.

"Can I stay home from church to finish my homework?" *No*.

"Can I meet some friends and hang out at their house?" *No*.

"Can I sign up for soccer *and* karate lessons?" *No*.

"Can I have a computer in my bedroom?" *No*.

"Can you get me a _____ for Christmas?" *No*.

As a parent, there are often times you need to say no. Resist the urge to be the "party" parent whom they adore for the moment because you just gave them something they really want. Often the things they want—smartphones, iPods, or other technology—will actually isolate them from the family. That will only make your job of parenting harder in the long run.

A word of caution here. As a parent, there are often times when you'll need to say *yes*. Sometimes kids just want Dad to play or help them with something. Many times dads say no without thinking. Maybe they're busy on their computer. E-mail. Facebook. TV. Smartphones. Objects that have become their electronic idols. They're distracted with something that doesn't exactly hold eternal importance. Or maybe they just don't feel like doing whatever the kids are asking them about.

Sometimes I hear parents saying no when their kids ask something that is totally appropriate. I stand there thinking, why *not* do that with your kids? Are you even listening to them? They're asking you to do something that good parents are *supposed* to do.

I know. You're tired. But don't be a lazy parent. The kids just want a little time with you. The day will come when they won't need that anymore. Why rush that time of life? So don't brush them off with a quick *no*. Find an alternative and you'll all be happier.

Creative alternatives are especially important as the kids get older.

"Some friends are going to meet at _____'s house to hang out. Can I go?"

Truth is, your gut says no. You don't know who is going to be there, what kind of supervision they'll have…and that's just for starters. But give an alternative.

"No, I can't let you go to her house to hang out, but you can invite your friends here. I'll even spring for pizza."

Yes and no. Two of the simplest words in the English language. But if you use them wrong, you're going to complicate your marriage and your parenting. Count on it.

Keeping Yourself
Out of Ditches

To develop and maintain a solid, loving, Christian marriage—and to raise kids who grow to love the Lord in the process...*that's* our destination as husbands and dads. We can have the best of intentions, but that doesn't guarantee we'll reach that destination. The road of life is treacherous, and many marriages end up in the ditch.

I want to give you two tools to help you reach the destination of being a great husband and dad—to do the types of things I'm suggesting throughout this book. The two tools are *self-control* and *Holy Spirit control*. These are my two hands on the wheel. The more I practice self-control and Holy Spirit control, the better I'll be at staying on the road and out of the ditches.

Tool One: Self-control

In exercising self-control we choose to do things the right way. God's way. The Bible often refers to that as *dying to self*. This means we have to put in some effort. We fight. We stay on guard. We don't make excuses to act however we feel.

> Like a city whose walls are broken through is a person who lacks self-control (Proverbs 25:28).

In Bible times, the walls around a city were all about protecting the people inside from attack. From raiders who would come in to steal or destroy. People in a city with broken walls were vulnerable. Easy prey. A man living in a city with broken walls couldn't protect himself or his family. The parallel to us today is obvious. If we lack self-control, we're living in a very dangerous place.

- A place of vulnerability.
- A place where someone can steal from us.
- A place where we can get hurt.
- A place where we can't protect ourselves—or our family.

If we live without self-control, in a city with broken walls, we're putting everyone we love and everyone who loves us at risk.

Lack of self-control gets people in trouble all the time. Think about the nasty things that cause trouble in our marriages, families, and even in our world.

- Problems with selfishness, pride, anger, and unforgiveness.
- Problems with jealousy, lust, and fear.
- Problems with reckless talk, addictions, and bad habits.

All these and more are results of a lack of self-control. Broken-down walls leave us and those we love vulnerable to the enemy.

Self-control has a lot to do with doing the right thing, even when you don't feel like it. It's about acting and reacting according to God's Word. And self-control isn't something we can pull out of our pocket whenever we need it. It takes work. It's a discipline we *develop*. We make doing the right thing a habit—and eventually it pays off.

> Self-control has a lot to do with doing the right thing, even when you don't feel like it.

Tool Two: Holy Spirit Control

As Christians we can do more than just "white-knuckle" our way through life, trying to exercise self-control. We have the Holy Spirit to help us. We give him permission to change us. We ask him to kill our selfishness. And as we die to self, we're left with the new nature.

The Holy Spirit can change our attitudes and our hearts, if we let him. And one of the fruits of the Holy Spirit is self-control. As we give ourselves over to the Holy Spirit, our heart changes and he gives us *more* self-control. Things that'll protect us and those we love.

Use the two tools or not—it's a decision you must make. You either choose to pursue self-control and Holy Spirit control, or by default you'll be controlled by your natural desires. By your flesh. Which simply means you'll generally do what you feel like doing and say what you feel like saying, regardless of whether it is right or wrong. Regardless of whether it is wise and loving or not.

Many, many married couples miss this. They run on the default setting and never reach the levels of satisfaction and contentment a marriage can bring. They settle for something less. Mediocrity.

Electrocuting Pickles

There's a great illustration I like to do with groups to help illustrate this whole self-control and Spirit control thing. Imagine a lamp cord with the plug on one end, but on the other end, I've separated the two wires in the cord and twisted each of them around a nail. Now, I put electrical tape around both nails to keep the wires securely in contact with the nails. Next, I slide a nail into each end of a pickle, careful not to let the nails actually touch each other. Are you with me so far?

Imagine the pickle is you. One nail is your old nature. The other nail is the Holy Spirit in you.

Now, when I plug this thing in, you'll hear the pickle start sizzling immediately. And then the pickle lights up. It flickers and glows like a battle is going on inside. It's an amazing sight. I can stop the battle inside by unplugging the pickle or by carefully removing one of the nails from the pickle.

In the same way, a battle of conflicting desires often rages in us. There are things we'd like to do, but we know they're wrong. If we give in to the desires, we're bombarded with guilt. Our old nature is at war with the Holy Spirit and the new nature he's developing in us. It's a battle—and that's an uncomfortable place to be.

> The flesh desires what is contrary to the Spirit, and the Spirit what is contrary to the flesh. They are in conflict with each other, so that you are not to do whatever you want (Galatians 5:17).

When we unplug—when we die—the battle is over. But what about in life? Must it always be a battlefield?

No. There are two ways to end the struggle. You can pull either nail out of the pickle.

Most go for the easy option. They ignore the Holy Spirit. They rationalize. Compromise. Justify their behavior. They quench the Holy Spirit, and as they do, the battle subsides. This is choosing the broken wall option. This is the option that will result in your living in a city without walls. You'll be vulnerable. You'll be risking your marriage and your kids. You'll be sacrificing a closer, more meaningful walk with God.

The other solution is to join forces with the Holy Spirit.

You exercise self-control. You ask the Holy Spirit to change you. One battle at a time, you fight back the old nature. And as you do, you find peace, joy, love, and contentment. This is an absolute key to life. A key to a great marriage. A key to successful parenting. A key to living a Christian life that is real—not fake.

Self-control and Holy Spirit control are the keys to doing everything I've written about in this book. Everything. Let me try to illustrate how this works. There are times where my attitude is off. I'm irritated about something. Let's imagine I'm upset with something my wife did or said, or maybe it's something she didn't say or do—but should have, in my opinion.

Now, I can brood about that, and it will end in conflict. It will result in blowing the night with her. I can come up with a list of reasons that I'm right and she's wrong, but there's a problem.

Am I acting in love? *Maybe in self-love.*

Am I keeping a list of wrongs? *Definitely.*

Am I loving her like Christ loved the church? *Probably not.*

But I can't seem to turn my attitude around. And the truth is…part of me doesn't want to.

Here's where the choice comes in. I can let nature take its course. The old nature, that is. And I'll make a mess of things—guaranteed. Or I can ask God for help. That part takes a little self-control, right?

When I feel my attitude is going south, I've learned to drop to my knees in another room. I confess what I'm feeling. I confess that part of me doesn't want to straighten things out—because I feel I'm justified to a certain extent. Then I ask the Holy Spirit to change me. To change my heart. My perspective. To see things the way I should as a Christian man. I only take a minute to do this.

And generally within a minute or two I can already sense my perspective changing. My frustration dissolves. The building anger loses steam. It's beyond explanation. And I know it's God.

As a result of me using a little self-control to ask the Holy Spirit to control me, the time together with my wife turns out to be excellent. What might have turned into an argument and a wasted night turns into a great time together. Now I rarely even have to slip into another room to drop on my knees. When I feel my attitude souring, I shoot up a silent prayer giving permission for the Holy Spirit to change me—and he does.

This is how you're going to be the man, the husband, and dad the Word explains we should be. **Exercise self-control to give the Holy Spirit control.**

This is powerful stuff. It builds walls of protection around you, your marriage, and your kids. Do you realize how freeing this is?

When I'm speaking to groups I like to have three volunteers come up for a little race. I hand a roll of toilet paper each to two of them. They need to unroll the TP without ripping it.

When I feel my attitude is going south, I've learned to drop to my knees in another room.

Then the third volunteer works with me. We'll have to unroll two rolls of TP, too, but we'll do it together—and in a little different way. I challenge the first two to beat us and I even give them a head start.

Now, as the first two volunteers are furiously dumping toilet paper on the ground, I pull out a leaf blower and hand it to my volunteer. I've modified it with a small paint roller bolted at the end of the air nozzle chute. I load the first roll of toilet paper and turn on the blower—and the paper flies off the roll. In about ten seconds the first roll is gone— shooting across the room in one continuous stream. The first two volunteers are still working away while we load and empty the second roll of TP with the modified leaf blower.

The volunteers emptying the rolls by hand are like most of us. We go through our Christian life doing our best—working hard and trying not to mess up. **But we'll always be limited living this way.**

God has a different plan. He gave us his Holy Spirit to work powerfully in and through us. To change us if we let him. Like that modified leaf blower, God helps us in unexpected ways to change and do things we could never do on our own.

You may feel like the first two volunteers I had. Working hard. Trying not to mess up. You may read things in this book you don't think you can possibly do. News flash…you can't. God never intended you to do this on your own.

If we want a marriage that is going to be exceptional, if we want a marriage that will reflect what a Christian marriage is all about, we need to understand that **we can't do it on our own**. God didn't design it that way. The same goes for parenting. We use a little self-control to ask for Holy Spirit control. We give him permission to change us. And he does things we can't foresee, predict, or even imagine—just like those volunteers never guessed I'd use a modified leaf blower to beat them.

The Holy Spirit isn't a bully. He doesn't push himself on us. We ask for his help. We give him permission to change us. And as he does, and we recognize it, we draw closer and closer to him—and our walk grows more and more real and successful.

So I say, walk by the Spirit, and you will not gratify the desires of the flesh (Galatians 5:16).

It is the combination of self- and Spirit control that will...

- help you be a doer of the Word, not just a hearer.
- keep you from saying unkind things to your wife and kids.
- keep you from bad attitudes or pull you out of them.
- rescue you from selfishness, pride, anger, and bitterness.
- protect you from temptation and lust.
- release you from prisons of addiction.

If you were driving a treacherous road and the conditions were bad, you'd have both hands on the wheel...right?

The road of life is treacherous. Self-control and Holy Spirit control are my two hands on the wheel. They're going to help me reach my destination and keep me out of the ditches. Buckle up and try this—and you'll enjoy the drive.

Muscle Cars and Marriage

I had the privilege of growing up in the day of the true muscle car. Deep rumbling big-block engines rolled off American assembly lines. Firebirds, Camaros, GTOs, and Vettes. Chargers, Barracudas, Chevelles, and Cobras. Mach 1s, Trans Ams, 442s, and Road Runners. Lots of makes and models. Great machines that burned gas and rubber as fast as they went from 0 to 60.

There was an aura about these cars. Still is. Seeing one of these muscle cars today gets my heart racing more than a brand-new car possibly can.

My brother-in-law, Duane, had a dark green 1970 Mach 1 with a four-barrel 351 Cleveland and a four-speed Hurst shifter. The deep rumbling sound of that engine was enough to get any guy's adrenaline pumping.

For me, it was the Firebird Trans Am. My midnight blue T/A had a massive 455 cubic inch V-8 with a four-speed manual transmission. Fast? It was the closest thing to a rocket I'll ever drive.

Duane lost his Mach one foggy morning in a bad accident—totaled in a collision with a Corvette. Two sweet muscle cars to the junkyard in one horrendous moment. And I sold my Trans Am shortly after getting married. The truth is, most muscle cars didn't make it. They wore out, rusted out, or got wrecked along the way. Which is why the good ones are worth so much today.

Which brings me to marriage. Most women wouldn't appreciate

being compared to a muscle car, but hey, there are a couple important parallels.

First, not many marriages last—and many that do aren't in great shape. Every couple goes into marriage wanting a great one. Few will work at it. They'll run it into the ground over time. Like a car towed away by the auto wrecker, many marriages end up on the scrap heap.

Second, if a car is going to go the distance, it needs regular, preventive maintenance. If you're smart, you don't wait for a car to break down before you fix it.

A few years ago I noticed a little rust spot on my wife's car. It was inside the gas cap compartment—I couldn't even see it from the outside. I could have fixed it with a piece of sandpaper and a bit of touch-up paint. No problemo. But I didn't—and the rust spread onto the rear quarter panel. Not an easy fix anymore.

Men, the same principle applies to your marriage. You need to maintain it. Your wife may not tell you when something is wrong. You have to listen to her tone of voice. Watch her eyes. Body language. Do you sense hurt there? Frustration? Fear? Anger? Discontentment?

You'll want to pay attention to where she's at—to the things she says and the things she *doesn't* say. If something isn't quite right, figure out how you can help or what you can do—before it's too late. You need to hear what's on her heart. What's important to her. It's about valuing her.

A lot of guys I knew abused their muscle cars when they were younger. They drove hard and fast all the time. Eventually they stopped thinking their car was so special. They went on to other cars. Other interests.

You have to be careful to always treasure your wife—which won't come naturally. She's not always going to seem so special to you. You'll be tired, or she will be. But don't take your wife for granted. She's been entrusted to you by God on loan. She's there to love, encourage, and help you. You're to help, protect, and love her. That takes deliberate action and dedication on your part.

My brother-in-law would love to have his Mach 1 back. And I'd love to have that Trans Am in the garage. In fact, lots of guys pay huge, ridiculous bucks to buy muscle cars. They keep gaining in value.

If you maintain your marriage right, it will keep gaining in value too. It'll stand out in contrast to all the mediocre marriages out there. It'll bring both of you untold satisfaction. Guys would pay a million bucks to have a marriage like that—and they could have had if they'd paid more attention to the details as they went along.

And treating your wife right will get you some extra mileage when it comes to parenting. That example you give to your kids is powerful. They'll respect Mom more because they see *you* do. Your kids will see you demonstrate how a man should treat a woman. That will put them miles ahead of others when they get older.

And if you have daughters, it's a great way to protect them, too. They'll see how a woman should be treated, and when they get older, they'll be less likely to get trapped in an abusive relationship.

So treasure your wife. Give your relationship all the attention it needs. Don't wait for problems to develop—and when you see a problem, don't procrastinate. The benefits for parenting are obvious…and the payoff in marriage is priceless. Treat that girl right and you'll both find marriage is a great ride.

Two Ways Women Need to Be Shown Affection

Sorry, guys, we're not talking about sex here. But if you get these two things right, it can definitely lead to good sex. There are a couple of ways most wives want love *shown* to them by their husband. Undivided attention...and a little public display of affection.

Undivided Attention

The term *multitasking* actually sounds like a good thing. Like we're being good stewards of our time. As a kid I used to practice the piano in the basement—right by the TV. After school I'd watch *Gilligan's Island* while I fumbled at the keyboard. Even though I was proud of my dual accomplishment, the quality of the music I played proved multitasking has its limitations.

Today's technology fuels multitasking like never before. People use these techno-tools and toys while they're driving, working, talking to someone else—you name it. In this busy world, you may feel you need to do a certain amount of double duty in order to survive. Just to get the essentials done. That's probably true.

But there are dangers if we don't get really single-minded and focused at times. In marriage, doing more than one thing can *multiply* our problems—especially if it's while you and your mate are talking.

Focus total attention on your wife when the two of you talk.

Men and women think differently and process things differently—and misunderstandings happen easily. Truth is, we need all the help we can get. When we look at our wife when she talks, we have a much better shot at understanding what she's saying…and what she's not saying. Her body language and facial expressions are a big part of that.

If you're checking e-mail or texting while the two of you are talking, you're sending your spouse a message too.

- I'm too busy to give you my undivided attention.
- This conversation isn't important enough to warrant my full focus.
- I'm not that interested in what you have to say.
- I don't need to give you 100 percent. I'm a good listener at 80 percent.

But if you want your wife to feel totally secure, you need to give her your total attention. Not every time you talk. It just isn't possible. But you need to carve out time when you just talk together. Time when you totally listen to each other.

This is one reason I go on a weekly date with my wife. Usually we sit across from each other at a fast-food place and catch up. We have each other's undivided attention. A couple times I brought my computer along—and regretted it. Most technology ends up being a distraction.

Imagine a college basketball player with a phone in his hand, texting someone while running down the court during March Madness. That divided focus would *truly* be madness. He needs to keep his head in the game. Now think how much more important your marriage is. It's a high-risk, high-stakes venture. The payoff is huge, too, if you do it right.

When you're preoccupied with anything else, she'll sense that. That won't make the fiber of your marriage stronger. It will unravel it. You won't be able to read her as well. You may miss something in her expression, in her eyes, that she isn't saying verbally. Sometimes she won't be able to express how she feels. You'll have to figure it out. And it will take every bit of attention you can give. Even when my wife calls on the phone, I've learned I need to step away from my computer. I need to focus on what she's saying.

I know men who were self-absorbed multitaskers. They got a lot done, but they lost out with their mate. They were checking their e-mail when they should have been watching their wife's eyes. If they had done the right thing, they would have seen the changes going on long before the divorce papers came. In my opinion, they missed their window of opportunity to fix something. By the time they found out, it was too late for talking. Or for listening.

Imagine how a man would feel if he was making love to his wife and right in the middle of things she picked up the phone and texted a friend. How satisfying would *that* be to the guy? It would be an insult. He might get discouraged and feel like his wife didn't love him, or maybe he'd get hopping mad.

And who would blame him? Men rank sex right up at the top of things that are incredibly important to a marriage. Well, women consider communication and listening with undivided attention to be incredibly important elements of a great marriage. It tells her just how much her husband loves her. So if a man is distracted while his wife is talking, it will affect her badly—just as it would him if she were making phone calls or checking Facebook while they were having sex.

This whole listening thing is so huge it's scary. Incidentally, that's often how men lure women to cheat on their husbands. They listen. They give a woman their full attention—something they know women hunger for. They're users, and they're looking for easy prey—which is exactly what a woman can be if her husband isn't a listener.

Be sure you're dedicating time daily to really listen to her. How do you want her to listen to you? Treat her the same way. It's a rare quality in this multitasking society—and one that will pay back well if you put it into practice.

Kids Need Undivided Attention Too.

As dads, the good habits we establish by limiting our multitasking with our spouse will pay off big with raising kids, too. When they're little, it means getting down on their level. Listening to what they're saying or trying to say.

Listening to your kids is part of being a good parent. When you stop what you're doing and really listen to your kids, you're communicating some critical things without saying a single word—that you value them and what they're thinking. Parents are often concerned that their kids develop a healthy sense of self-worth. Kids with a low sense of self-worth are less secure and are at risk in ways that others aren't. Parents often go to great lengths to build a sense of self-worth in their kids. Often they try to do it by getting the kids involved in confidence-building activities—like sports. Don't miss the greatest, sure-fire way to build their sense of self-worth: Listen to them.

Consider making mealtime a media-free zone. No TV. No phones. No computers. Just focus on communicating with the people right there in the room with you. As they get older, you'll need to have all your senses engaged just to be sure you're hearing what they're saying. Many parents miss the nonverbal cues that would tip them off to something critical with their kids. Deception. Lies. Anger. Hurt. Pain. Fear. Loss of respect.

If they don't think they have your attention, likely they'll clam up. It's not that they'll stop talking…they'll just stop talking to you. They'll find someone else who listens. The problem is, that will often lead to more trouble. Don't let that happen to you.

Multitasking husbands and dads tend to think they're pulling it off. Getting two things done at once. Back when I watched *Gilligan's Island* while playing the piano I was proud of myself. But I didn't do nearly as well at the piano as I could have. I didn't reach my potential. I didn't really make music.

That's the problem if you multitask while you're supposed to be communicating with your wife or kids. You're going to miss some things—and that can make all the difference. You're smarter than that. So keep your head in the game. Turn off your phone. Stay focused on each other when you talk and you'll make beautiful music together.

A Little P.D.A

A second way women need to be shown love is through a consistent and appropriate public display of affection.

Sure, we all remember times when a couple showed too much passion to each other in public. A school hallway. Riding public transportation. On the street. At times the whole thing crosses boundaries of affection and looks a whole lot more like lust. Moms cover their kids' eyes. Wives glare at their husbands if they find them staring.

There are certainly times when a public display of affection is in bad taste. The problem with most married couples is that they run the other way. They don't show *enough* affection in public—and that will negatively affect their marriage and the kids.

When you're married, you *need* to show a little P.D.A. I'm not talking about the types of things that make people suggest you get a room. Showing appropriate affection—even around your kids or others—is more than okay. It's essential.

P.D.A. says good things to your mate.

It *shows* you love your spouse—which beats just *telling* your wife you love her. It's all about the way you look at your mate, the way you find opportunities to smile at her. To get close. To touch her. Showing affection says things like…

"I'm glad you're mine."

"I like being with you."

"I'm happy I married you."

Think that will strengthen your marriage?

P.D.A. communicates all these and other good things women need to be assured of—which makes them feel more secure. It does for my wife. Insecurity has so many bad side effects, and a little thing like P.D.A. can help prevent it from taking root. It's medicine. In Song of Songs 2:4 the woman says, "Let him lead me to the banquet hall, and let his banner over me be love."

Let his banner over me be love. That's classic P.D.A. in action. A public place, and the man's affection is as evident as a banner hanging over her, announcing *this girl is loved!*

- Hold your wife's hand.

- Put your arm around her.

- Give her a hug—and don't let go too fast.

- Kiss her like her lips are magnetic—quick to draw you in and hard to pull away from.

- If you're a nuzzler, bury your nose in her hair and draw in the scent of her.

- When you say goodbye before work, pretend she's deaf and blind. Which means you'll hug her and kiss her in such a way that she feels your love.

When I say goodbye to my wife on the driveway and she starts worrying about neighbors watching, I know I've shown her how much I love her, how much I want to see her again, and how much I'll miss her while we're apart. Not a bad way to start the workday.

Guys, with a little P.D.A. you're protecting your wife from predators. Other men. The low-lifes who prey on women who don't get enough affection from their husband. Women who don't feel loved are more vulnerable to "charmers"—guys who will make women feel good about themselves.

Actually, P.D.A. protects both of you. A wedding band tells others you're married. But the truth is, a lot of people don't care about the wedding band. They'll flirt and charm and try to seduce anyway. P.D.A. sends a message on top of the wedding band. It says, "We're *happily* married. We're off the market." Not a bad safeguard to have in place, don't you think?

And P.D.A protects your wife from other dangers. Often women who don't feel appreciated at home look for affirmation someplace else. They put in extra effort to affirm their worth, their husbands get the leftovers…and the marriage takes a hit. If you're careful to show her love, she'll be able to hold her head up and won't need to look to others to make her feel special.

One more thing, guys, and this one is subtle. With frequent P.D.A. you're telling your wife that you're interested in her—*all the time.* That you like to be with her. Close to her. You're always stoking the fire of love. Why is that so important? Because when it comes time to go to bed, sex will simply be a natural progression of what's been going on all day.

Often you'll hear women say something like "He's only interested in me when he wants sex." They may be right—or he may be really distracted during the day. Whatever the reason, the results are the same. Women tend to resent that. Feel used. And they generally find ways to get that point across in the bedroom—which doesn't help their marriage much either.

A guy who doesn't pay much attention to his wife throughout the day and then wants some good loving at bedtime is settling for microwave sex. Instantly hot and not all that satisfying. I'm a big fan of slow-cooker sex. My wife often makes some kind of pot roast dinner in a slow cooker. She keeps the heat on low all day and the aroma fills the house. It totally builds the appetite. That's the beautiful thing about P.D.A. Pay attention to your wife whenever you see her during the day and you'll build some anticipation. And then when it's time for bed, both of you will be ready.

P.D.A. says good things to your kids.

They need to see Mom and Dad love each other. A rock-solid marriage is a source of security for them. And the more secure home feels, the better off they are.

Now, as the kids get older, they may moan and complain that they don't want to see the hugs and kisses. The times you hold each other for more than two seconds and whisper something in each other's ears. Too bad. Do it anyway. There are worse things than our kids thinking that a Christian marriage works. There are worse things than our kids thinking passion in marriage doesn't fade when we do it God's way.

Another big payoff for kids? They get a view of what a healthy marriage should look like in action. If it doesn't look like the two of you share any real passion, why would you expect them to ever talk to you about sex? They'll think you're clueless. They'll ask others their questions. Hiding your affection when the kids are around is a big mistake. Gigantic.

P.D.A. says good things to others.

A little P.D.A. in public is often a good example to others. People at church. People you mingle with socially. In this world of mediocre marriages, you'll be a reminder of what marriage should be like, and *could* be like when it's done God's way. Even your kids' friends need to see what it looks like to love your mate. They may not see it at home, and somebody needs to model a healthy relationship to them. Show your wife you love her, and she'll find ways to do the same for you. P.D.A. is one of the secrets that make a marriage soar above the level of mediocrity out there.

I married Cheryl because I loved her so much that I wanted to be with her all the time. I enjoyed being together. And I still do. P.D.A. helps keep it that way.

For a better marriage that also benefits your kids, work hard to show your wife you love her in a couple of ways she needs it most. By the way you listen to her with undivided attention and by showing her affection—in public.

Help Your Wife, Help Yourself

D r. Kevin Leman, a Christian psychologist, wrote a book years ago entitled *Sex Begins in the Kitchen*. The premise was that satisfying sex was a natural by-product of a good, caring relationship lived out throughout the day. I've heard women rag about their husbands and how they can be oblivious to their needs until they want sex. Then suddenly they become real helpful.

One aspect of a good, caring marriage is *helping* each other. Women generally have a better handle on that than men do. They tend to sacrifice more to help their husband than the other way around. And realistically, some men simply don't have time to do much more than they're already doing. But there are usually ways to be more of a help to your wife, even if you don't have much time. Here are four principles to help you become a truly helpful husband.

Find ways to lend a hand.

Lighten her load. This is basic, but it's also important. The kitchen work isn't just the wife's job. Rarely do I leave the kitchen without staying until all the dishes are cleared, rinsed, and loaded in the dishwasher and every crumb is wiped up. We're in it together.

Most of the time you'll know what needs to be done. Jump in before she gets exasperated and asks for help. If you wait, your efforts to help at that point won't be seen in the same positive light.

Sometimes you'll need to *ask* how you can help her. If you notice she seems overwhelmed, that may be a real clue that she could use a hand.

Do what she wants you to do the way she wants you to do it.

When we had our first son, I started helping with laundry. Often I'd sort, wash, dry, and pile it up for her to merely fold and put away. She flat out told me she'd rather I didn't start the laundry if I wasn't going to fold it. Leaving it in a heap, even though it was clean, wasn't helping her at all.

I thought she was exaggerating. I mean, hey, I sorted, washed, and dried it. How was that *not* a huge help?

The answer was obvious. I wasn't doing it her way.

After doing enough laundry over the years, I learned she wasn't overreacting at all. I'd rather rewash a pile of clean laundry than deal with all the wrinkles after being heaped up like that. But even if I'd never realized she was right, I'd still need to do it *her* way. If my motive is to help her, then doing the job the way she wants it done will be the biggest help to her. If I take the attitude of "Well, she should just be glad I'm helping her," I am missing the point.

You probably have a routine going in your marriage as to who does what. Great. But don't think your job is done when you've finished *your* list. Help your wife with *her* list as well. When you're careful to help her, even when you're busy, you're communicating things essential to a good marriage. "We're in this together—you're not alone." "You're so important to me that I want to help you. I appreciate all you do for me."

Do whatever she needs you to do as soon as you possibly can.

Write it down so you don't forget. Don't procrastinate. You might say, "I'm too busy right now." Here's how she hears that: "You're not that high on my priority list."

Incidentally, sometimes men complain that their wives nag too much. Remembering what she needs done and tackling it as soon as possible make it harder for a woman to resort to nagging.

Do it without grumbling or complaining.

There will be some things a woman wants done that seem ridiculous. You may feel you have a lot more important things to do. But remember this: Whatever it is she wants you to help with is important to her. If you complain about doing it, you'll rob yourself of much of the appreciation—and reward—you would have gotten if you'd done it with a great attitude.

Think about it from a different perspective. Imagine there is something she really wants you to do for her or with her. Suppose you grumble, "I'm beat. I've worked hard all day." Most men feel justified in doing that. But what they can't understand is why she grumbles when he wants sex and she gives him the same lines. "I'm beat. I've worked hard all day." You want her to help you happily, even eagerly, in areas that you consider important—like sex. Remember that when she asks you to do things that are important to *her*. Treat her the way you want to be treated.

Not that you're doing all this for sex. Not at all. You're doing it because it's the right thing to do. It's part of being a good man and a great husband. In so many ways, when you're really deliberate about helping your wife, you're helping yourself at the same time.

And you're helping the kids. You're showing your daughters how a man ought to treat a woman. If she dates a real clod someday, she'll recognize it and be more likely to say *adios*. You're showing your sons how to treat a woman right. How to value her enough to help without complaining. And hey, if the kids are younger, get them involved.

"Let's help Mommy do _____."

"Let's surprise Mommy by doing _____."

You can do this. Help your wife, and you'll be strengthening your marriage and teaching your kids at the same time. Being a good husband really is the best way to be a good parent.

Okay. Enough already. You got this, right? Roll up your sleeves and get to work!

Stick with Scrabble

As a dad, one of my parenting "secrets" was to make a game of things. Whether it was encouraging my kids to eat their dinner or getting them up the stairs for bedtime, I often turned it into a game. It made things more fun for all of us. That's the way good games should be. They should make you laugh—make everyday routine things more enjoyable and fun.

In marriage, and in families, there are good games and bad games people play. Let's focus on two of the most dangerous "head games"—played even in Christian marriages.

The Silent Treatment

The rules are simple. The offended party shows just how hurt they feel, how angry they are, or how badly they believe they've been treated by clamming up. At its root, this game is about punishing the other party. If a wife resorts to the silent treatment, she'll make her husband *feel* how much he hurt her. She wants to be sure he feels *really* sorry for what he did.

Winning the game? There is no winning the game. It hurts both parties—and often the marriage. Sometimes more than we'd ever guess.

Often the person being "punished" gets angry right back. They retaliate by getting silent themselves. A vicious cycle—and deadly. Rarely does the silent treatment lead to positive or beneficial outcomes. Sometimes it leads to really, really destructive thoughts—like "I don't need her."

Guys, you'll be tempted to play this game. Don't. Establish new ground rules together. At the top of the list would be the rule that the silent treatment is not acceptable in your home.

The Cold Shoulder

This is another one on the nasty game list—and closely related to the silent treatment. This game is usually initiated by a husband or wife who is offended by what their spouse did or didn't do. You know how it works. It isn't as blatant as being completely silent, but it certainly is cold.

The cold shoulder is about using your words, actions, body language, and attitude to let your other half know that you've been wronged. One thing you can be sure of: Just like the silent treatment, you can't play the cold shoulder and still have a warm heart. Another name for a cold heart is a "hard heart"—and Jesus fingered that in Mark 10 as the root behind divorce. The silent treatment and the cold shoulder...dangerous games indeed.

★   ★   ★

Both games require unhealthy amounts of pride on the part of the person initiating them. The better you or your spouse are at playing Mr. or Mrs. Freeze, the more you can be sure there is a strong root of pride and selfishness behind it.

Once you roll the dice with either of these games, it gets more difficult to stop with every minute that passes. The heart hardens quickly, and the longer it goes on, the less your heart will want to stop. Often the game will be played right up until bedtime. The bedroom can become a kind of torture chamber to truly punish the spouse—and sex is the weapon. You either refuse sex or show such a coldness that the thought of making love becomes ridiculous. Any type of sex would be robotic—lacking all intimacy. Likely neither one of you wants to touch the other—or be touched. Talk about killing passion.

These games produce no winners. Only wounds.

Never use sex as a tool to manipulate or punish your spouse. That's *always* a bad idea—and will hurt the person trying to manipulate as much as the one deprived. It's hitting below the belt, and it weakens the marriage.

Think about the game of Russian Roulette. One bullet in a revolver, spin the cylinder, place the barrel to your temple, and pull the trigger. The game requires a lack of brains—and if it goes badly, ends with a bullet in the head. Now *there's* a game you'd never be tempted to play. Right? Well, anytime you resort to the silent treatment or the cold shoulder you're playing *relational* Russian Roulette.

These head games are forms of high-stakes gambling. It is allowing your own stubbornness and pride to put the health of your marriage up as the bet. It may end up weakening your marriage more than you can imagine. Some marriages will die during the process of one of these games and they'll never recover. It absolutely happens.

Now, think about what you're communicating as a parent. You're showing your kids that playing these games in marriage is okay for Christians. But the Bible tells us to do everything in love. Everything. And you can't play these games in love.

Maybe you think you can handle the game. But if your spouse or one of your kids is more sensitive than you, the damage this game inflicts happens quicker and cuts deeper. Recovery will take longer and may not ever be complete. Yeah, maybe you think *you* can handle it, but do you want one of your kids playing the same game in *their* marriage someday?

The games may be hard to stop, but they're easy to start up. The game can begin almost naturally with just the smallest steps. A wrong attitude can quickly become a twisted head game.

My strong advice to you is to avoid these games. Always. Actually, I'm begging you to avoid them. Think about how far off these games are from where a loving relationship should be.

These games have nothing to do with protecting and treasuring each other.

These games have nothing to do with building each other up.

They have nothing to do with helping each other become God's man or woman.

These games will teach your kids really lousy relational skills.

These games have nothing to do with Christianity.

These games are about inflicting pain and hurt on each other.

These games are stupid, but lots of couples play them.

Sure, there will be times each of you disappoint the other, hurt each other, and make each other hopping mad. Get a grip on yourself and ask God to change your attitude. Give the Holy Spirit permission to change your heart.

But don't play games. Even if your wife goes silent or cold, don't resort to doing the same. Be a hero. Then talk it out like the adults you are. Romans 12:9 says it well: "Love must be sincere. Hate what is evil; cling to what is good." Love is action. It takes effort. And if your love is sincere, it means you don't get to pick and choose which parts of your mate you'll love. She's a package deal. Sincere love doesn't have gaps. You love her on the good days and on the bad.

The word *cling* in the Romans passage has a sense of "hang on for dear life" urgency. The life of your marriage depends on it. So get a fresh, strong grip on your mate and God's principles for marriage. And hate—totally avoid—anything evil. And that includes the evil games couples play.

If you want to play games in marriage, stick with Scrabble. Or make games up yourself. But just make sure the games you play make you laugh, smile, and draw you closer to each other. Why roll the dice with anything else?

Hard Hearts

When I'm speaking to a group, I like to get a volunteer up front. We put on gloves and safety glasses, and they help me make a super cold slush by mixing acetone together with crushed dry ice. The volunteer buries a dill pickle and a hot dog in the –100 degree slush solution.

Two minutes later the volunteer uses a pair of tongs and pulls the pickle and hot dog out. I hand them a hammer and they give the pickle a whack. It shatters and flies in all directions. The same thing happens to the hot dog.

Combining the right ingredients creates a solution that will freeze things rock-solid in just a minute or two. Something pliable, like hot dogs or a pickle, becomes rigid. Something that normally bends will break. Something that would normally shake will shatter.

This can be fun to mess with, but there's a very chilling parallel to the Christian marriage. Daniel tells of King Nebuchadnezzar's great power and success…but goes on to tell about his downfall.

> When his heart became arrogant and hardened with pride, he was deposed from his royal throne and stripped of his glory (Daniel 5:20).

Pride is a key factor to make a heart hard. Just one chapter earlier Daniel warned Nebuchadnezzar to turn away from what he was doing wrong. Apparently he did not. Nebuchadnezzar didn't follow God's obvious commands—even though he knew better.

And this is a second factor to make a heart hard—**willful disobedience.** Simply ignoring God's Word. Disregarding what it says. Or having an attitude that *I'm entitled to special rules just for me.*

When you combine pride and willful disobedience, you create something very cold and sinister. And it doesn't take long. A heart can harden in minutes—I've seen it. Sometimes the briefest comment—or even the tone of voice—is all it takes to start a heart hardening.

Jesus tells us in Mark 10:1-12 that the root of divorce is hard hearts. It's the root of a mediocre marriage, too. Not all mediocre marriages end in divorce, but in a very real way they end in another way. What does a hard heart look like?

Where you were once pliable, you become immovable.

Where you were once flexible, you become rigid.

Where you were once caring, you become insensitive.

Where you were once convicted, you feel no shame.

Where you were once kind, you become rude and critical.

Where you were once patient, you become short and irritated.

Where you were once concerned about your mate, you become focused on yourself.

Where you once sought to understand your mate, you argue your position.

Where you once sought truth, you deceive yourself to believe a lie.

I've never had a volunteer offer to put their finger in that super cold slush for two minutes. It would be insane. Dangerous. Ridiculous. I imagine an unprotected finger would freeze solid and shatter just like the hot dog. If you dipped your finger in that solution you'd sense the danger and pull it out of there immediately.

Hard-heartedness in marriage is just as dangerous.

Maybe you're proud. You consider yourself more important than your wife. You focus on your needs and desires instead of hers. Or maybe you're willfully disobedient. You don't live out God's Word even though you know better. You disregard God's principles for the way you're called to love your wife. Know this: Combining these two ingredients—pride and willful disobedience—makes a lethal combination. It's like sticking your marriage in the freezing solution. If you find yourself going there, turn around—and fast. Otherwise, you'll find that marriages can shatter just like that hot dog.

★ ★ ★

If your marriage isn't what it should be, you need to stop the argument over who is right and who is wrong. You need to grow up as a Christian. Protect your marriage and you'll protect your kids at the same time.

★ ★ ★

Sadly, hard hearts are incredibly common—even among God's people. I know couples who lost their marriage and (at least to a partial extent) custody of their kids in divorce. Their hearts hardened. And the results were awful. And preventable, if they had followed God's Word. These couples, and so many like them, settled for shattered lives—and their kids are paying the price right along with them. We must be on guard against hard hearts. Ask God for help.

Ask him to show you your pride. Attack it.

Ask him to show you where you need to obey better. Then follow God's Word, regardless of whether or not your wife does.

Ask him to keep your heart from hardening and to soften it where it is already hard.

Maybe you and your wife are having problems right now. Imagine the two of you arguing on your driveway while your kids are playing by the curb. Suddenly, a car pulls up and two men jump out. They grab your kids and start dragging them to the car. What would the two of you do?

You'd stop the argument immediately and rush to save your kids. Suddenly all your differences would be meaningless compared to your kids' safety. You'd fight to the death to protect them.

If you're getting sloppy with your marriage, that's exactly what's happening. While the two of you are arguing, while you're focused on yourselves, your kids are in real, grave spiritual danger. We have enemies out there—the devil and his demons. They would love to steal your kids away from you and the Lord.

If your marriage isn't what it should be, you need to stop the argument over who is right and who is wrong. You need to grow up as a Christian. Get rid of the pride. Commit to live God's way. Protect your marriage and you'll protect your kids at the same time.

It was a frigid January night in Chicago. I was at the airport waiting outside by the curb for Cheryl to pick me up.

A woman came out of the terminal and stood about five feet away, waiting for her ride. Clearly not dressed for Chicago winters, she hugged herself and turned to me.

"It's cold as hell here," she said.

I thought that was an odd statement. The words *cold* and *hell* didn't seem to fit together. But when I think about that dry ice demo, and the parallel to hard hearts, maybe her statement wasn't so far off.

Cold, hard hearts—they really do come right out of hell. Just like the cold shoulder and the silent treatment. And as a Christian, you don't want any part of it in your life.

God designed marriage to be incredibly valuable. A factory of blessing that stays profitable and keeps providing. Don't let a hard heart bankrupt you. Fight it. And see how rich your marriage can really be.

Wearing the Pants

In 1979, pop singer Neil Diamond introduced "Forever in Blue Jeans." He sang about being content with simple things like wearing blue jeans and being with the girl he loved. I can identify with that. I love taking my wife on a date, and when I do, I'm usually in a pair of well-worn jeans. Soft. Comfortable. The way blue jeans should be.

But some blue jeans are stiff and coarse. Picture a brand-new pair of deep indigo jeans—not the prewashed type. Imagine wearing them on a ten-mile hike on a sticky hot day. Totally uncomfortable. Definitely not the kind of jeans I want to wear.

Leadership and submission in marriage are supposed to be as comfortable as those prewashed jeans. But many women see submission as a source of conflict and irritation. It chafes at them—which makes this issue one of the trickiest minefields a man will navigate as a husband. But we're going to look at God's plan—and see how well it can really work.

Good leadership as a husband is about balancing things out so that you don't become some kind of pigheaded power-monger on the one hand or a jelly-spined pushover on the other. One is just as bad as the other. Both of them are equally twisted perversions of God's plan. A husband who succumbs to either of these extremes can be described by the same word. *Loser.* A man who lives in either extreme is going to lose God's best for him in marriage, and his wife and family will lose right along with him.

Cheryl and I agreed from the start that I would "wear the pants" in the family—in the spirit of God's plan. It's one thing to say it, and another to do it. Over thirty years later I can say that she certainly kept her end of the bargain. I consider her to be the absolute expert, the *best* at what healthy submission looks like.

God's plan is pretty simple. He is the head—of all of us. But organizationally, his plan calls for the man to lead the wife, and for the man to take his cues from God. As the husband, you're the ultimate decision maker. Which also means you will ultimately be responsible to God for the decisions you make. So when you make a call on something, you want to do it carefully. You need to consider what you feel God wants you to do. In light of that, you have to do what you believe is best for your wife, your family, and you. Sometimes that won't be what any of you really wants.

I live in a suburb of Chicago. Not exactly an area known for integrity in politics. A former governor made national news in allegations of using his authority to gain advantages for himself. It was a corruption of power. Despicable. And it's just as bad when a husband wields his authority for selfish reasons.

Most of the time my wife and I are really good at making decisions together. Weighing all the facts. Trying to discern what God would have us do. Searching our feelings, convictions, and Scripture. Ultimately, the decision rests with me. Not that I point that out to her. We just both know. I don't try to pull rank on her just to meet my selfish agenda. When she sees I am careful to do what I think God wants me to do, it is easier for her to trust me. And the more she trusts me, the more carefully I want to make my decisions. I don't want to let her down. I don't want to mess up on my responsibility to God. I don't want to make a mistake. When we do it right, God's plan works really well.

My wife is a great resource for me when it comes to decisions. She has that "women's intuition" thing going for her, and sometimes I think her sensitivity allows her to hear the Holy Spirit sooner or more clearly than I do. As a result, she's helped me make many, many great choices. I'd be stupid not to consider her thoughts on an issue.

But she isn't always right. Nobody is. And men, your wife won't always be right either. You'll have to think, pray, and do what you feel is best.

Be careful of trying to manipulate your mate in order to get your way. Men sometimes do this by intimidation. By bulldozing their way through. By throwing their weight and authority around. If I went around like some little dictator I'd be a first-class idiot. The picture we have in the Bible is Jesus. Sacrificial, loving leadership. A man who follows Jesus's example finds the whole issue of leadership and submission ceases to be a conflict. So if the two of you are having a conflict, one or both of you aren't doing it God's way.

Think about it. What woman in her right mind would have a problem following a man who knew his place under God, a man who sought to make decisions for God's glory and his wife's good? A wise woman can't help but show love to a husband like that. And as she does, her husband is all that more determined to do the job right.

Sure…there will be times you make a wrong decision. When you realize it, admit it. When I make a bad decision, Cheryl doesn't rub my nose in it. She knows my heart, and we're a team. And I love her all the more for it.

The picture we have in the Bible is Jesus. Sacrificial, loving leadership.

Side by Side

My dad's uncle, Billy Arnold, won the Indy 500 in 1930. Back then, two men rode in the car—side by side. The driver *and* the mechanic. Both indispensable—but very different roles. The mechanic helped keep everything working right. He was an extra set of eyes and ears watching for threats, danger, and opportunities. Billy didn't grab the wrench and the mechanic didn't grab the wheel. Billy didn't have to remind his mechanic who was driving. They didn't fight each other. They were a team. They relied on each other. They valued each other. They won or lost together.

This is a great picture of the roles of husband and wife. Billy Arnold didn't win the Indy 500 by having a power struggle with his mechanic.

And no couple is going to finish well in marriage without a clear handle on how the roles of man and wife were designed to help and complement each other.

Marriage is a two-seater racecar. You're the driver. Your wife is like your mechanic. God designed her for her role. Gifted her for it. Don't put her down. She's not your enemy or your competition. She's your teammate. Remember, without her you can't succeed in having a good marriage. This race takes two.

Don't micromanage your wife. Don't always be telling her how to do things "right." Don't constantly correct her because you want her to do everything your way. In other words, don't grab the wrench. Let her do things her way. Let her use her head. Let her be creative.

So lead well. With compassion. Helping her. Growing her. With God's will and her well-being at heart. Sometimes that will mean making some tough calls. There will be times when it will mean your wife will be nudged out of her comfort zone. Becoming the woman God meant her to be may require some real stretching. God is counting on you, men, to do it right. Your role isn't simply to "transform" her into a better wife for *you*. You are to help her become the woman God intends her to be.

How stupid would it have been for Billy Arnold to try to do everything? What if he hadn't let his mechanic help as much as he could have? Get your wife's input. Her opinion. Listen to her. Chances are, she's going to see things you don't—both dangers and opportunities. The race takes two.

★ ★ ★

Your role isn't simply to "transform" her into a better wife for *you*. You are to help her become the woman God intends her to be.

★ ★ ★

Get this right and you'll find out just how great marriage can be. You'll enjoy each other more, and you'll be modeling something for the kids that most never see. You'll be impacting the next generation in gigantic ways.

A servant leader must take the lead in a balanced way. He must be careful not to become a *dictator* or a *doormat*. Sticking to God's plan is critical for the success of your marriage and your family. Remember Psalm 127:1: "Unless the LORD builds the house, the builders labor in vain." Be careful to do it God's way and acknowledge God in the process. As you do, your wife will come to trust you more and more.

Cheryl made it clear right up front that she wanted me to wear the pants in the family, and she teased that as my wife she could pull them down whenever she wanted. Works for me. Leadership and submission has become a very comfortable arrangement for us. Neither of us would have it any other way. Not because I'm so smart, but because God is.

Like a stiff pair of unwashed jeans, submission and power struggles chafe away at so many marriages. Jeans weren't designed to chafe and irritate the people who wear them. When I'm dressed up, I always love to get home and throw on a pair of jeans. The longer you own them, the more comfortable they feel.

And that's sort of how a good marriage feels. When you do marriage God's way, leadership and submission work together as comfortably as a pair of well-worn jeans. And that is my hope for you—that you'll join me forever in blue jeans.

Surviving the Storms

Growing up, I spent the better part of my summers at my folks' summer home at Lake Geneva. I loved watching storms howl down the lake, kicking up white-capped waves and churning up the bottom.

We had a regular routine to keep everything safe and undamaged. We'd hustle to close the picnic table umbrellas and get the covers tied on. We'd winch my dad's boat into the boathouse. Loose items on the dock got stowed or tied down tight.

When storms hit at night I never had to get up to check the waterfront. We made sure everything was "storm-ready" before we went to bed for the night.

Some storm preparations were done well in advance—like with the floating raft anchored thirty yards offshore. Every spring we'd inspect the anchor chain for wear and replace all the cotter pins on the shackles—whether they seemed to need it or not. When a storm had that raft heaving and bucking at that anchor, we were glad we did.

You'll have plenty of little storms in your marriage. Squalls will blow up—sometimes without warning. Sometimes it will be circumstances. Loss of a job. Health issues. A family crisis. Other times the storms come in the form of a disagreement or argument. There are times when you get frustrated, angry, or exasperated with each other.

Storms can be really destructive if you aren't prepared. I remember seeing boats that hadn't been tied well in their dock slips. Sometimes the waves pounded the boats against the dock, doing nasty damage to the hull. Others swamped, and in some cases, sank.

The same thing can happen in marriage. Let's take a look at ways you can come through the storms without your marriage or kids taking a hit in the process.

Be Prepared

Talk about how you intend to handle differences and arguments. By working some things out in advance, there'll likely be less damage done during an argument.

Also, realize your family life was probably quite different from your wife's. There may be some things she'd do or say in an argument that are completely normal to her but really hurt you—or vice versa. Often these types of things don't belong in a solid Christian marriage. We talked about some of these earlier, like the cold shoulder and the silent treatment. You could probably add plenty of other things to these two. Like making rude, hurtful comments to each other. Sarcastic remarks. Insults. Leaving the room—or the house. You'll have to work out how the two of you intend to handle disagreements and arguments. It's best to do this before you're in the middle of the storm.

Avoid the Storms When You Can

My dad used to wear dark, wrap-around sunglasses when he drove the boat. He called them his "storm-finders" because the lenses made it easier to see rain coming. When a storm started blowing in the distance, we didn't sit in the middle of the lake and wait for it to hit. We'd race back to the dock and get the boat and everything else tucked away safe before the storm thundered in.

Sometimes in marriage we get an early indicator that a storm is brewing. You can often avoid a lot of needless hurt and damage if you handle those things quickly—before a storm hits full force. What types of things are likely to turn into a storm? Financial issues? Habits that irritate each other? Make some personal changes now and you may avoid storm damage later.

Fights in a marriage can lead to good changes, but fights are never necessary for change. It's much better to talk issues out before they ever escalate into a storm.

Attack the Storm, Not Each Other

I remember one time the raft broke loose in an especially violent storm. Made of solid wood with Styrofoam floats underneath, that thing was heavy—especially after being in the water for weeks. You can imagine the damage it could do to our dock or the boats moored nearby. We acted immediately. I threw on my mask and fins and pulled the raft against the waves to keep it from destroying anything. Everyone available helped, and it took those combined efforts to get the raft safely in place. Imagine if we'd stood there arguing, throwing accusations at each other as to whose fault it was. Instead, we attacked the problem to protect things from being destroyed.

The same thing can happen in an argument. The focus can shift from fixing the *problem* to fixing the *blame* on each other. In the meantime a lot of damage can happen. When some people argue, they never get past the accusations and insults.

When you do have a difference of opinion, try to get to the heart of it as quickly as possible. Sometimes that means you have to listen—without interrupting—so your wife can vent. Often the root issue doesn't come out right away. Maybe it's a really old wound that needs cleaning and healing. The first things you hear may just be the symptoms. Even when you're pretty sure you understand what's bothering your mate, you may want to repeat it back to her just to make sure you're interpreting things right. Often you'll find there is something more, something deeper.

It's easy to match insult for insult. Easy to do—but *stupid.* You're hurting the one you

★ ☆ ★

Fights in a marriage can lead to good changes, but fights are never necessary for change. It's much better to talk issues out before they ever escalate into a storm.

love, even though you may not feel so loving at the moment. You're damaging yourself—your own relationship. That's like a person who puts a fist through their wall in anger. Now they have more repairs to do.

Conditions for Storms Are Perfect

Here in the Midwest, sometimes we'll get a "tornado watch" warning scroll across the bottom of our TV screen. The weather conditions are perfect for a storm. The networks try to warn us to be extra careful and watchful—for our own protection.

There will be times in marriage where the conditions for an argument are heightened. You're tired. Consumed by busyness. Discouraged. Feeling like a failure. Discontent with some aspect of life. Frustrated by circumstances. Starving for intimacy. Longing for escape. Relief. Those are the times you need to be careful to pull together so you don't drift apart.

Going Out in the Storm

When a storm hit at the lake, we didn't go out in the boat or take a swim for fear that lightning might strike while we were vulnerable in the water.

I'd highly advise you both agree that you will never leave the house angry. That neither of you will storm out of the house to clear your head, get away from each other, or whatever. That is cowardly, and is usually a thinly veiled excuse to punish the other person. To show just how mad you really are. Maybe to even scare your spouse a little.

Think about it. You're anything but clearheaded, driving in traffic with your mind totally someplace else. Not much different from driving drunk. The chance of an accident is high. And if you walk out on your wife in anger, you may undo years of trust. It communicates something you really don't want to say. It makes your love look very conditional. "I'll always love you, and I'll always be here for you, unless I get hopping mad at you. Then I'll do whatever I feel like doing. And that means I might even bolt right out of the house." Not exactly hero stuff.

Men, sometimes that's enough to make women lock up part of their heart, never allowing themselves to trust too much or love too much for fear that it will only hurt more when it is taken away. You don't want that. You need to stick with her—no matter what. If you need some space, go to a different room for a while, but don't *leave.*

I know a man who left—but when he came back found his wife was gone. And she didn't come back.

The damage walking out does to kids is even worse. It gives them a lousy example of how a Christian man or woman should act and it erodes their security. If they see Mom or Dad walk out, they'll never be sure if they're coming back. Love your mate, love your kids, and love God enough not to leave the house.

Talk to each other about what it would say to each of you if the other one walked out in anger—even to cool down. Leaving the house is dysfunctional—plain and simple. You don't want seeds of it in your marriage. If you've ever done this before, this would be a good time to confess, tell your spouse you're sorry, and commit to handle it differently in the future.

One side note. I'm not talking about a case of physical abuse here. If you're physically abusing your wife, or verbally abusing her, get help. Now. Because she has every right to walk out if you do that—and she should. You'll lose everything you care most about in this world if you don't fix this. I've seen it happen. And when it does, it happens fast, hard, and often with no second chances.

Storms Blow Over Quickly

Or at least they're supposed to. I've seen storms pass us at the lake, circle around, and take another swipe at us. But I've never seen one last for days and days. How freaky and unnatural would that be? Same with arguments. Generally speaking, get them over and done with.

Cheryl and I took Ephesians 4:26-27 quite literally.

> In your anger do not sin. Do not let the sun go down while
> you are still angry, and do not give the devil a foothold.

We both knew there was a time limit on our anger—we'd have to work it out before we went to sleep. And that was a healthy thing. We talked it out and usually resolved things. I could probably count on one hand the times we let something go until the next day. Generally those were times when we were so tired we couldn't be at all productive in our talk. Then we'd both agree to delay it until the next day—but no longer than that. You never want to let something go indefinitely. Anger is a demon in the house. You want to get it out of your place quickly.

Sure, once in a while there will be an issue that will circle around like a storm and hit again. There are other issues you'll tackle on and off for years. But as each incident comes up, deal with it and be done with it—fast.

Cleaning Up

When a storm hit the lake, rarely did we have any real damage because we'd prepared in advance. There were usually messes afterward, though. Branches, leaves, and seaweed and dead fish along the shoreline. We cleaned up every reminder of the storm, and everything looked good again.

After an argument, there are some little cleaning up issues as well. Saying things like "I'm sorry," "I was wrong," and "Will you forgive me?" go a long way toward cleaning things up. Also talk about how you can avoid similar arguments in the future.

Sometimes you'll feel you were 100 percent right on an issue. There are times I felt that way. But then I had to look at how I handled everything—including the argument portion. Was I kind? Loving? Even though I may have believed I was right, all too often I *handled* it wrong, and I had to clean that up.

Lose the List

When it's over, it's *over*. The Bible reminds us not to keep a list of wrongs. If you find yourself saying things like *You always...* or *You never...* you're likely keeping score in a bad way. If you bring up past failures you're keeping a list of wrongs—and that's never right. When Jesus forgives us, he doesn't keep a record and constantly remind us about it. Don't do that to your mate.

Have you ever put a CD in a microwave oven? You've got to try this. Take a CD and put it on a plate with the label side up. Set the timer for six seconds—*no more than that.* Turn it on and watch. You'll see flames and sparks as that CD short-circuits itself. After it cools, take it out of the microwave and you'll see a bizarre-looking spiderweb pattern etched across the CD. That CD that once held a ton of information—books' and books' worth of data—can't be played again. All the info, all the data, is gone.

That's a picture of the way God forgave us. When he forgives, it's like he nukes the CD that records our sins. He'll never replay it. Never hold it over your head. And *that's* the way we're to forgive our spouse—and our kids.

Do you have a tendency to bring up your wife's same old sins? Grab a blank CD, write her name on it with a marker, and whatever the situation or "sin" she committed below it. Don't get too specific when you're writing down her sins or that storm may circle back. Microwave it and give it to her with your full and genuine forgiveness. "I'll never play that back to you again."

Storm Chasers

Ever see one of those programs about people who go out in their teched-out van *looking* for storms? They look for tornadoes and twisters, try to get close to them and take pictures. In my opinion, these are people who headed a few too many soccer balls as kids.

In a similar way, there are some people who are just looking for a fight in marriage. I've seen couples start sparring while we were with them. Totally awkward. Talk about being off the bubble when it comes to a good marriage. Their whole perspective was out of whack. Couples often treat arguments like some kind of competition. Like it's a wrestling match or something. Instead of points for a "takedown," they score points by a well-timed "put-down." Tragic stuff. They're hurting themselves.

You've seen it too. Couples launching insults at each other in public. Imagine what happens in private. A married couple shares the same boat, whether they like it or not. When they lash out and attack each other they're drilling holes in their own boat. That's dangerous. Wrong. Foolish. Selfish. Proud. And when kids get hurt because of it—that just multiplies the tragedy of it all.

Remember, the devil and his demons are out to get you and your kids. Be really, really careful how you handle anger. And get it out of your house fast—like Ephesians 4:26-27 warns us. You *do not* want the devil to get a foothold in your home. How scary is that thought? The enemy is not your spouse, but the forces of darkness that would distract you from living God's way, from living according to God's guidelines.

Fights are very, very dangerous. Don't go looking for one. I think Romans 12:17-18 says it pretty well. "Do not repay anyone evil for evil. Be careful to do what is right in the eyes of everyone. If it is possible, as far as it depends on you, live at peace with everyone."

I pray your storms are few. And I pray you and your mate will prepare for the storms to minimize any damage, and that you'll work together during the storm so you come out of it stronger and more committed to each other than ever.

* * *

The Elephant in the Room

Let's face it. Sometimes there are issues you have with your wife that need to be addressed. If you want to avoid future storms, there needs to be a change. Maybe you've talked about it before, or maybe you haven't. But it's always there, never out of sight.

Sometimes for the sake of your marriage, the kids, or maintaining a Christian testimony there are times you need to confront your spouse. Like an elephant in the room, the issue just can't be ignored.

Philippians 2:14-16 reminds us to "Do everything without grumbling or arguing, so that you may become blameless and pure, 'children of God without fault in a warped and crooked generation.' Then you will shine among them like stars in the sky as you hold firmly to the word of life." With that in mind, exactly how do you deal with the elephants in the room? How do you confront in a proper way?

Understand why you're confronting.

A good spouse confronts to bring out the best in their mate. Confronting is about changing a course of action or behavior. **It is about making your future together better—not about winning an argument.**

Let that last statement sink in a bit. If you're out to prove a point, show you're right, or win an argument—that's *all* you'll accomplish. You probably won't see any real change. If you go into it like it's a fight, you'll probably get one. You'll end up with a nasty argument and you'll both be hurt. The elephant will still be there, and soon you'll be back to swinging a coal shovel to clean up the messes.

There's a biblical pattern for confronting. Pull out your Bible and read two passages. First, the story of Abigail confronting David in

1 Samuel 25. Read the whole chapter. Take note of how Abigail defused a deadly, volatile David and turned the situation around.

Next, read chapters 4 through 7 in the book of Esther. Pay close attention to how Esther turned around a pompous, egotistical king and got him to effectively undo an unalterable ruling he'd made.

Drop a bookmark here, close this book, and go to *the* Book. You may feel you remember the stories well enough—but read these passages again. Then come back and we'll talk about confronting successfully.

The right start is critical.

Did you notice that Abigail and Esther didn't go in to win an argument? They weren't satisfied with being "right." They had much bigger goals. They wanted to effect a change.

David and King Xerxes both made poor judgments. Bad decisions. Both were on their way to making a big mistake. Both Abigail's and Esther's future would be affected by the men's actions—this wasn't going away. The stakes were high. If David wasn't stopped, he would've killed Abigail's husband and the men who served him. Likely more family would have been caught in the slaughter. Her future would have been ruined along with her husband's. If King Xerxes wasn't stopped it would mean the death of Esther's beloved cousin, her relatives and countrymen…and quite likely herself.

Both Abigail and Esther approached the men with total humility. Which had to be hard, right? The men were being clods. But these women weren't out to win an argument. A true "win" in their book would be nothing less than seeing the men making a real change. A heart change.

Both women took a huge risk confronting the men. Abigail rode straight into an angry army. Esther broke protocol—a breach that could have ended her life.

Both women brought something to the men. Abigail brought much-needed food for David and his men. Esther threw a banquet for the king—which totally appealed to his big ego. She pleased him, and teased him by initiating a second banquet before she'd even tell him her request.

Both women approached the men in a respectful and humble way. They didn't come looking for a fight. In fact, the way they approached made it look like they wanted a favor. And remember, these men were both in the process of making big mistakes in judgment—yet the women still showed incredible respect.

Neither of the women accused or blamed the men. They put the blame where it belonged. Both David and King Xerxes were victims in their own way. David had been dishonored. Xerxes had been duped. Their actions weren't good, but the women could empathize enough to see the men weren't villains.

Both women urged the men to make a change. Abigail urged David to take the high road. To do the noble thing. To do the thing that would please the Lord. She helped him guard his heart, his reputation, and his future. Esther urged Xerxes to come to her rescue. Both women helped the men see the long-term consequences of their action.

Both women provided a way for the men to save face. Abigail provided food, making it no longer necessary to take it by force. Esther came up with a legal plan to allow King Xerxes to effectively nullify his earlier edict to exterminate the Jews.

Both women saved the day. They got through to the men. They confronted the men so well, so strategically, that the men changed their course of action, and it changed the future.

Both women impressed and pleased the men so much that the men wanted to do more. David ended up marrying Abigail. King Xerxes wanted to give Esther up to half of his kingdom.

Guys, you can learn a lot from women—and that includes wise women like Esther and Abigail. Sometimes you need to confront. It's about stepping alongside your wife to help her change the future for both of you. It's helping your wife by bringing out the best in her. Give the matter thought and prayer before you jump in and sound off.

- Confront with humility—even if you feel she's totally wrong and you're right. God's Word tells us we should confront in love. Be very careful about confronting in anger or some kind of holy huff.

- Be kind, and be mindful of your mate's ego. Remember, rude, critical, self-righteous, and sarcastic approaches rarely do anything but make matters worse.

- If possible, pick a time that isn't so emotionally charged. Abigail didn't have that luxury, but she did great anyway. Esther did have more time, and she used it well.

- Pick a place that will give you enough privacy and limited interruptions. And as a general rule, confronting in front of the kids would *not* rank especially high on the smart-o-meter.

Is there an elephant in the room? You need to do something about that. Elephants belong in the zoo or the circus—but definitely not in your marriage or home. You don't want to keep cleaning up those kinds of messes.

When you're ready to tackle the topic, you need to think hard about what you really want to accomplish—and how to do it. Are you going to confront just to show they're wrong and you're right? You're shooting too low. Learn from Abigail and Esther. Don't confront to merely win an argument. Confront to effect a change, save the day, and prevent storms. The choice is yours.

The Truth About Lies and Secrets

ruth and honesty. As men we need to fight for these. They are critical to all areas of life—especially in our relationship with God. He makes that pretty clear in the Bible. God hates lies and deception. Honesty is essential for a good marriage—and for solid parenting. Dishonesty is breaking trust, isn't it? And if you erode trust between you and your mate, or you and your kids, what do you have?

A first-time parent will shoot a video to record their baby's first words. They'll snap pictures of their first smile. They'll cheer at their first steps. And they'll grieve at their first lie.

It's devastating. Seeing that little child lie to your face rips you apart. And deep down you're asking yourself, *Why?* Why did they feel they had to do that—to *me?*

Lies are part of our natural man. As old as the Garden of Eden. As sharp as a dagger—and able to penetrate the heart in the same way.

People try to minimize lying. Sometimes they use harmless-sounding names. Whoppers. White lies. Fibs. And a person who is lying is simply bamboozling you a little. They're kidding. Joking. Fudging. Exaggerating. Telling a fish story. Being tactful.

Generally people lie for four basic reasons.

1. To avoid something uncomfortable or unpleasant. Many times it's about being tactful—like telling someone what you think they want to hear. Let's say you meet someone you haven't seen in a while. The years haven't been kind to them. But of course you don't say that. "You look great. Have you lost weight?"

2. *To avoid punishment or consequences.* You messed up. Did something that will get you in trouble. So you decide to cover it up. "It wasn't me. There must be a mistake." There's a mistake all right. And you just made it by lying. This is about avoiding something that is deserved.

3. *To protect someone—usually ourselves.* Sometimes lying can appear noble—especially when we tell ourselves it's to protect someone. But honestly? With a little thought you can usually find a way to do it without lies.

4. *To get something they wouldn't get with the truth.* Often lying is an attempt to gain an advantage or a privilege a person isn't entitled to. It's deception for selfish motives. It's the salesman promising something he knows his product won't deliver. It's the "charmer" telling a girl anything—just to get what he wants. "Of course I love you. And I want to show you how much." This type of lying is about getting something that is undeserved—something they'd never get if they told the truth.

Lies are all about self-love. About getting something I want, but don't deserve. About avoiding unpleasant consequences I do deserve. About making things more convenient or more comfortable for me. At its very root, lying is putting my wants, needs, and desires above what is right and wrong. No wonder God hates it so much.

Honesty is about loving others. Proverbs 24:26 says, "An honest answer is like a kiss on the lips." Think about it. In Bible times a kiss on the cheek was a way of greeting someone. It was polite. A formality. A courtesy. Probably a lot like how we'd shake hands with someone today.

But to kiss someone on the lips? That's a symbol of love. The meaning is clear: **Honesty is an act of love.** An honest answer is the most loving answer I can give someone.

Honesty and Our Family

We want to be honest—and teach our kids to have the integrity, the character to do the same, right? This is what's best for our marriage and for the kids. Lies destroy trust. Honesty builds it. Let's make an effort, a commitment to be honest. All the time.

Watch the little things. The phone rings and your kid reads the name on the caller ID display. "It's Uncle Harry."

"I don't have time for this. Tell him I'm not home." *Oops.* Didn't you just tell your kid that lying is okay when the truth isn't convenient?

Watch the big things. There are all kinds of lies husbands and wives tell each other. So stop it. Make a decision. Love your mate enough not to lie to them. Love your kids enough not to tell them lies, either.

Example A: Mom and Dad's marriage is fine.

Some couples have a mediocre relationship. The fire they once felt for each other has long been extinguished. But they know that their kids can be hurt if they know that. So they put on a façade. They put on an act that things are okay.

Some take it to a deeper, darker level. They want out—but they don't want to hurt the kids. They want a divorce, but decide to wait until the kids are off to college. They feel this is the more noble thing to do. The right thing. The honorable way. When the kids are old enough and emotionally mature enough, *then* they'll drop the bomb. They'll bust the myth. Then they'll get the divorce.

Wow, what a nifty plan.

Mom and Dad give each other plastic smiles and steely cold hugs. Kids may hear arguments, but Mom and Dad assure them later that everything is fine. Good even. Relieved, the kids buy the lie. Later, when the kids are off to college, one of the most critical times of their life—when kids decide to follow the faith or leave it behind—*then* Mom and Dad will pull the rug out from under them.

Gee, how noble.

This is lying to the kids—in a really big way. Put your efforts into fixing the marriage, not into carefully deceiving your kids. Hiding the problems instead of truly fixing them is not noble. It is not honorable. It is hypocrisy. A lie.

Example B: "You can be anything you want in life."

Parents say these types of things all the time to their kids. This kind of encouragement suggests that if a kid tries hard enough, he can attain anything. It's a message that kids interpret something like this: *As long as I don't let others hold me back, there are no limits to what I can achieve. I just need to work hard. If I believe, I can achieve.*

But it isn't true. I mean, really. Be honest. Our kids may be good in sports—but will they really be able to win Olympic gold or go pro? The vast majority will never make it. It isn't simply a matter of believing more or trying harder. There are other factors like gifting and ability that come into play as well. There are only so many seats on the pro sports bus, and the odds against our kids making it are high. Yes, some will make it, but most won't.

If we use these clichés with our kids they get the message that (1) they can map out the plan for their life, and (2) within themselves they have the power to carry it out. *They're* the captain of their ship. *They* determine the direction their life is to go.

For Christians, the truth goes beyond the "believe and achieve" clichés. The truth is found in God's Word: "For we are God's handiwork, created in Christ Jesus to do good works, which God prepared in advance for us to do" (Ephesians 2:10).

Often those things God has planned for our life won't be accomplished solely with human effort. He wants us to experience something more. He gives us things to do that are beyond us. Things we can only do if we learn to trust and rely on him. Things we can manage only if we're doing it with God's wisdom and power. There are many passages in the Bible that help us understand this.

It all boils down to this truth.

God has a plan for your kids' life.

God has some things he wants them to do.

God generally makes the task bigger than they can handle so they learn to trust him—not so that they simply try harder or believe more in themselves.

With all this in mind, let's make a subtle but more *honest* correction to the old parental cliché: *With God's help, you can do anything God wants you to do—no matter how impossible. With God's help, you can become anyone God wants you to be—no matter how improbable.*

The key is the emphasis on God's plan, not our own. We are not the captain of our ship. We want to plug in to God's plan—and get his help to accomplish it.

Honesty is no excuse to be abrasive. How does the old saying go? "Tact is telling someone where to go so nicely that they actually look forward to going there." The point is you can speak the truth in love, just as the Bible tells us to. Use tact. Watch your tone. Muster up some empathy. That takes effort. Careless, cutting "truth" is kind of lazy, in my opinion. Find a nice way to say things, even if the truth you have to say is hard.

Lies must be confronted. Whether it is your spouse or your kids, don't let lies go unchallenged. Handle it in private. Talk with your kids and show them that lies are wrong and they always make things worse. And if it is your spouse doing the lying, talk together about taking the high road. About having a marriage that is honest.

When it comes to your kids, don't be naïve. Young, sweet, innocent kids lie through their baby teeth—and often about small issues. Be a detective. Check up on your kids. If they're lying, you want to catch it early so you can work on correcting the behavior. "But won't it look like I don't trust them?" Maybe. Explain that you *do* trust them. But as a good parent you need to check at times to be sure you can *keep* trusting them.

What About Secrets?

Some secrets just shouldn't be told. I saw a TV program once about some lame-o who revealed magicians' trade secrets and demonstrated how the illusionists did their stunts. The guy masked his identity—and for good reason. I'm sure some professional illusionists would've liked to make him disappear for good.

Movies and TV shows often show the trouble couples get into when they keep secrets *from each other* or tell secrets *about each other* that they shouldn't. The shows are produced to entertain—to make viewers laugh or cringe. But in real life mistakes like this can be tragic.

Cheryl and I developed a formula when it comes to secrets. We don't tell people secrets *about each other*, and we don't keep secrets *from each other*.

Things to keep secret

The longer a man and wife are together, the more you'll know about each other. Each other's fears. Failures. Embarrassing moments. Times one of you acted like a bear or a baby. You'll know all kinds of little secrets about each other—which is just the way it should be. And these are the kinds of secrets that are meant to *stay* that way. These are secrets to keep from the world outside your marriage.

My wife and I made this commitment to each other early in our marriage. *We wouldn't share secrets about each other to anyone.* That meant when we were at some event and she saw me talking to other guys, she knew I wasn't talking about her in some bad way. She had the confidence I wasn't sharing something that would overly embarrass her. If she saw me talking to my folks she knew I wasn't ragging about her.

It turned out to be a smart commitment to make to each other. It built trust. Eliminated suspicion. And it saved us from a little stress and worry. Your wife needs to know her secrets are safe with you. That you won't go using her embarrassing moments to get laughs from others.

Now, I've told funny things about my wife, and she about me. Sure, we tease each other publicly, but we've drawn some lines we won't cross. And if we do cross a line, we talk about it, apologize, and don't make that mistake again.

I've known women who griped about their husband to her parents. Long after she kisses and makes up, a smoldering resentment still burns in the hearts of her parents. Complaining like that hurts a marriage. The only valid exception to this I can think of is if you need to seek some counsel on how to deal with a situation for the purpose of strengthening your marriage. Nothing wrong with that.

I've known men who tell intimate little secrets about their wife— right in front of her. Of a time when their wife was especially amorous or something. It made him feel like a man to tell others about it, but it embarrassed the wife. Of course, he's the real loser in the deal.

In her heart she probably promised herself never to let herself go like that again. He got some laughs but lost some loving. I'd call that a poor trade.

Things not to keep secret

I know couples who have secret bank accounts their husband or wife doesn't know about. Worse yet, some have secret lives.

Cheryl and I don't keep secrets from each other. It's the ultimate accountability because it touches every aspect of life. If I consider doing something wrong, I picture myself having to tell my wife about it. If it would disappoint her in some way, it's easier for me to do the right thing. My commitment to be completely honest with her helps me keep living right.

My wife can look at my e-mails anytime. She can play back my phone messages. She can listen in on any conversation I have and I won't be embarrassed. Why? I don't keep secrets from her.

When it comes to our jobs, my wife and I have different circles of friends. Not that we'd have reasons to keep secrets here, but I deliberately try to draw her into my world, and she does the same for me. I know the names of the people at her workplace and the names of some of their kids. That helps me understand her more.

There are only two types of secrets I'll keep from my wife. One is when I'm told something in confidence that I shouldn't share with her. There are things I'm privy to as an elder that I just can't talk to her about—and won't. The other type of secret is when I'm planning to surprise her in some way—like with a gift.

Secrets and Your Kids

This principle is exactly what you want to teach your kids. From a young age we talk about the kinds of secrets that are proper to keep, and those that are not. There are family secrets that should not be told outside the home. As parents, we patiently help our kids discern the types of things they can tell others about and those that they should hold in confidence.

Tattling is another topic completely. Often, when kids are young, tattling is all about petty little things. The tendency is to tell our kids not to tattle. While it makes sense on one level, it is slightly off the bubble, too. The issue isn't the tattling so much as the heart behind it. If your son tattles on his sister just to get her in trouble, you need to deal with his motive as well.

If we forget about the heart and keep drumming in the "don't tattle" principle, we may also be hurting ourselves in the future. What if your daughter plans to sneak out to a party that could get her in real trouble? If your son is aware of it, you *want* him to say something to you about it. But if he thinks it's tattling—and therefore bad—he may keep his mouth shut. He'll even cover for her.

This is a fine line, I know. But if you teach your kids to talk to you if they're concerned about something their sibling is doing, and not just to get them in trouble, you'll all be better off. It's a heart issue.

Teach your kids how to keep secrets. I often told my boys special plans I had for their mom, whether it was a present or a special surprise. Sure, I was excited, and it allowed me to tell somebody, but I was really training them how to keep a secret and how to make marriage fun.

Teach your kids not to keep secrets from you. Help them recognize deception. And at a young age you need to help them understand that it's never okay to keep a secret from you because some other child or adult told them to. This is all about their protection.

Be careful about keeping secrets from your kids—often under the guise of trying to protect them from unnecessary worry or fear. Sometimes parents try to shield kids a little too much—or they sugarcoat the truth. We were very open with our kids. We told them of work problems, problems with others, and age-appropriate basics on all kinds of things. Being open like this helps kids learn how to process and deal with all kinds of issues. If it was an issue we needed to keep in our little family, we told them right up front. I can't think of a time they didn't honor that. It was good for them to see how we were asking God for help and bringing our cares and problems to him. Kids tend to trust that Mom and Dad can handle anything, so it's good and healthy for them to see where we draw our strength.

There are times in families where you need to keep secrets and times when you shouldn't. But it all starts with the two of you and the decision you make regarding secrets. This little "secret formula" Cheryl and I have has worked well for us, and I intend to keep living that way.

Your mate needs to know her secrets are safe with you—and that you aren't keeping secrets from her. Do that for each other—and you'll both have something to smile about.

Fight for Honesty

We need to fight for truth with all our strength. It isn't always easy, but it's totally doable. Honesty is the mark of a man. A hero. Guys—let's be truthful. One hundred percent. With our mate. Our kids. God loves it, and it is a way for us to show love. I'm committed to being honest with Cheryl. It's like a kiss on the lips—and I'm always up for that.

The Whole Truth About Sex

Sex is beyond words. One of God's masterpieces of creation. It's an absolute wonder. Proverbs, the book of wisdom itself, stutters when it comes to summarizing it. The verses below suggest that sex is one of the wonders of the world that we can't logically break down into a simple explanation.

> There are three things that are too amazing for me, four that I do not understand: the way of an eagle in the sky, the way of a snake on a rock, the way of a ship on the high seas, and the way of a man with a young woman (Proverbs 30:18-19).

These verses say to me that sex is right up there with the fascination of flight, the wonders of nature, and the freedom of sailing. Sex is listed here among some great ancient mysteries. How does an eagle soar with nothing but wind beneath its wings? How does a snake, with no legs or hands, move so smooth and quick across a rock? How can a multiton ship float?

In all his wisdom, the writer couldn't quite get a handle on the wonder of sex—that kind of close, intimate relationship between a man and wife. He never quite got past the magic of it.

Sex between a man and wife simply cannot be boiled down to some mere drive or urge without severely cutting short the true capacity and potential of sex. If loving sex between a man and wife has the potential to be this amazing, this beneficial, if it can be powerful enough to rival the fascination of flight, you can be sure Satan will try to mess it up. And he's done a thorough job of it.

The point of this chapter is simple. To help you gain a healthy, truthful understanding of what sex can really be. If you and your wife really grasp the full extent of what sexual intimacy can do for you, you'll have much less conflict and immensely more enjoyment in marriage.

Does that sound like the kind of thing the devil wants? Of course not. Which is why this is more difficult than it sounds.

For a devoted Christian husband, sex is the ultimate expression of his love. Sex is an urge—yes. It is a drive—true. But that is only part of it…or should be. The reality is this. Sex is the one way a man can use his mind, his emotions, and his physical strength to express his love. It is showing love with his entire being.

At times a woman may feel that simply being held close is the ultimate expression of love. Often, just doing that will totally satisfy her. She may not understand why that isn't enough for a man. When a man *isn't* satisfied with that, it may lead a woman to the conclusion that men are driven by primal urges. No wonder women think it's their duty to ration out sex.

I've held my wife many, many times until long after she fell asleep. Sometimes she just needs that. But if she wants me to express my ultimate love, she understands that just holding her is like stopping short of the finish line. Cheryl and I joke that this is why the marriage vows have the line "to have and to hold." A man needs to "have" his wife. To love her with everything he's got. Then he is of a clear mind to hold her. Both husband and wife are satisfied.

Helping your wife understand how good and important it is for you to express your love through intimacy is critical.

- Your wife needs you to tell her you love her.
- She needs to *know* it's true.
- She needs to know that she is the only girl for you.
- She needs to know that you truly need her and draw strength from her.

- She needs to know that a hard day of work—of laboring mentally and physically—is worth it for the joy of being with her.

I imagine she'd never get tired of you showing her your love like that. Unselfish, loving sex says all those things and does so much for a good marriage.

Here are some things to describe what sex means to a man in marriage and how sex benefits both husband and wife.

Sex is like rebooting a computer to its default settings. It brings a couple back to a proper perspective, reminding them how much they love and need each other.

Sex is like pure sugar. It sweetens life. Makes the mundane elements of daily life worth enduring.

Sex is like a micro vacation—a total escape the two of you can take every night.

Sex is like a magnet—drawing two people closer than possibly any other thing on the face of our planet.

Sex is like a fire that melts away petty differences between a man and wife that can creep into a typical day.

Sex is like a soothing breeze that blows away the troubles of the day until they shrink in significance.

Sex is like a gift, a way to show just how much you appreciate each other.

Sex is like a buffet meal, enjoyable, nourishing,

and bringing health and strength to your marriage and love for each other.

Sex is like some kind of emotional fusion, bonding the two of you together and increasing the level of dedication you'll have toward each other.

Sex is like a protective shield, guarding your marriage and love for each other from every kind of attack and enemy infiltration.

Sex is like gravity itself, keeping you grounded and safe from flying off into the darkness of temptation so prevalent around us.

Sex has the potential to be so much more than simply a hormonal urge or drive. When both of you truly understand this and strive toward it, sex can be all the things I've mentioned and more. The writer of Proverbs 30 had it right when he used the word *amazing* to talk about "the way of a man with a young woman." Sex truly is a wonder.

Aspirin was widely advertised as a "wonder drug" when I was a kid. Initially its benefits were seen as being a universal pain reliever and fever reducer. Eventually aspirin proved it had benefits that far exceeded mere pain relief. It provided definite advantages to the human heart when taken regularly. In a sense, it can be a preventive medicine.

In some ways we can look at sex as the original "wonder drug." It can get your mind off the little pains in life. But as preventive medicine it can actually protect your marriage. Regular doses of good, loving sex keeps a couple's hearts soft toward each other. This is extremely important for a healthy marriage, because hard hearts lead to tragedy, disaster, and divorce.

If you want to help your wife understand how important sex is to you as a husband and to a strong marriage, you have to demonstrate

to her that sex is all these things. You can tell her your feelings—and you need to. But telling is not enough. Make sure your behavior backs up what you say.

For example, if you don't seem to have time for her, are preoccupied, not showing her affection or making her feel special during the day, but suddenly at bedtime you perk up and want sex…what do you think that will do for her opinion of what sex means to you? You'll come across like a self-centered clod.

If you're selfish with sex—not being careful to consider her needs, her pleasure—what do you think that will do for her opinion of what sex means to you, and what *she* truly means to you? You'll be reinforcing a wrong conclusion—that sex is just an act. That to you, sex isn't much more than a primal urge or a lustful desire.

If you give your wife that impression, she won't see sex for all it really is or can be. It won't hold the same importance to her. She may look at having sex as her doing some sort of favor for you instead of it being integral for the health of your marriage.

> The Bible tells us that love covers a multitude of sins.
> So does love*making*.

Guys, if you want to have a great marriage, if you want to have great sex in marriage, don't wait until bedtime to show her how important she is. Don't be too busy for her—even when you're really busy. Show her love in lots of little ways and when it's time for bed it will be completely natural to express your love through loving sex. Be a hero to her all day long, and at night she'll make you feel like one.

And after you've had sex stay close to her. Like a couple of spoons in a drawer. Hold her. Hold her hand. If you do, you'll reinforce the truth that sex is more than an act, an urge, or a drive. It is the ultimate expression of your love. It draws you close to your wife and makes you want to stay close to her.

This will all take time. You won't be a perfect husband and your wife won't be a perfect wife overnight. Be patient. Kind. Gentle. Strong. Don't get demanding with sex. That will only take away from it. Remember 1 Corinthians 16:14: "Do everything in love." Everything.

★ ★ ★

Be a hero to her all day long, and at night she'll make you feel like one.

★ ★ ★

Keep moving toward that goal even when it comes to sex. Treasure her. And guys, watch your hygiene. Take a shower. Brush your teeth. If she likes a smooth face—shave, too.

And don't expect sex in marriage to look like some romantic scene in Hollywood. Remember, these are men and women who are *coached*. They may make their love look passionate, but remember it is rehearsed. Scripted. Choreographed. The real deal isn't like Hollywood. Sometimes sex is clumsy or awkward or funny. Sometimes long and passionate. But more often married sex is quick and comfortable. And it always has the potential to do so much good for each of you.

When your sex life is good, a lot of problems in marriage just aren't problems anymore. And *that* will help you with parenting in a bazillion ways.

Help your wife understand the truth about sex, both by what you say and what you do, and you'll have a relationship that's more fascinating than flight and more freeing than sailing the open seas.

Getting the Frequency Right

I remember my first transistor radio. Not exactly high tech. Complete with a 12-inch antenna and an earplug, the radio only had a couple of controls. The off/on wheel also controlled the volume. Then by slowly turning the frequency dial I could tune it to any AM station I wanted.

Between the stations only two things existed. Dead air—pure silence—and static. When I dialed in perfectly to the right frequency, there wasn't a bit of static—only music and pure enjoyment.

There's a lesson in here for marriage, too. If you get the frequency of sex right (in other words, how often you enjoy it together), it can be a source of pure satisfaction and strength in your marriage. If you get the frequency wrong, it can lead to some dead, uncomfortable air in the house and can be the source of some real static and stress.

The Danger of Not Enough Frequency

As a couple you have to take to heart the warning in 1 Corinthians 7:3-5 that you don't deprive each other of sex except for one reason. Prayer.

Even for prayer you are not to abstain from sex unless you meet two qualifications.

First, it must be by mutual consent. You *both* have to agree to abstain. You both have to agree this is the course of action you want to take.

Second, it must have a specific time limit. It is not to be some kind of open-ended vague decision. The implication here is that you want to limit this time because of the danger of *not* having sexual intimacy together. This is so important, so straightforward, I'm going to write the verses out for you.

> The husband should fulfill his marital duty to his wife, and likewise the wife to her husband. The wife does not have authority over her own body but yields it to her husband. In the same way, the husband does not have authority over his own body but yields it to his wife. Do not deprive each other except perhaps by mutual consent and for a time, so that you may devote yourselves to prayer. Then come together again so that Satan will not tempt you because of your lack of self-control.

Notice why we're to be so careful about abstaining from sex with each other? Whenever we abstain we make ourselves more vulnerable to Satan's temptation. Why would we want to chance that?

The idea here seems to be something like this. If you're facing some big issue, some decision or problem that is important enough for you both to agree not to have sex but to devote yourselves to prayer instead, that's okay—but you need to be extra cautious. You'll be a target for temptation like you wouldn't be otherwise. Get back together soon before that happens. And the thing is, often when you're going through the tough times and facing the biggest decisions, that's when you need intimacy with your mate the most.

But What About Some Other Good Reasons to Abstain?

Let's look at some of the common reasons couples abstain from sex and briefly see if they're valid.

Too tired for sex. This is totally understandable. Life can get exhausting—especially when working, going to school, ministering, and parenting. But Scripture doesn't recognize this as valid—maybe because when we're worn down we're even *more* vulnerable to Satan. Remember this. Sex doesn't always have to be long. It can be as quick as five minutes. I think anybody has another five minutes in them—especially in light of the benefits sex holds.

Not in the mood for sex. This is completely understandable as well. Not feeling like having sex can be totally selfish or it can be based on some very justifiable factors. Again, the Bible doesn't allow for us do only what we *feel* like doing. Marriage is a commitment. It's valuable. And worth protecting.

Doesn't deserve sex. This is often absolutely true. Maybe a couple is having an argument or the husband has been a jerk. The issue here is bigger than whether they're having sex or not. Their marriage, or attitudes about it, are in the danger zone. They need to straighten up their relationship on all levels—sex included.

Monthly cycle. This one may be an exception, especially when you look at the Old Testament passages about abstaining from intercourse during a woman's monthly period. Yet the First Corinthians passage doesn't mention this. This is a significant oversight in light of the fact that one week out of every month can be "out of bounds" for this reason. Is it something that was assumed? A given?

Or maybe it's because there are ways a woman can still bring a man to a climax *besides* intercourse. A woman can still sexually satisfy her husband—even at this time of the month. So even during her period, a wife doesn't have to take a siesta from sex. And when she provides in creative ways like that she helps protect her marriage from Satan and reaps all those benefits of a great marriage.

When you get right down to it, there really are no scripturally valid reasons for abstaining from sex, other than for a limited, mutually agreed-upon time of prayer. Anything other than that is adding to or taking away from Scripture. And the thing is, it's really all for our protection and provision. It's God's plan.

So what is the right "frequency"? That is something every couple needs to work out. For some men this would mean every day. For others several times a week. It varies, and can change depending on what is going on in your lives at the time.

Men, there will be times when you need to exercise self-control. There are times you'd really like to have sex, but in light of being loving and understanding, you may abstain due to the situation. There will be times when she's really had a rough day, or you feel she really just needs to be held. You as the man need to be considerate and not selfish. Sometimes for medical or physical reasons sex isn't possible, but I believe God gives special grace in such cases.

Don't use Scripture as something to beat her over the head. Scripture is enlightenment. Truth. Work together toward getting the frequency right. But at the same time remember that abstaining from sex is always an *exception* to the norm. Be careful not to make such frequent "compromises" that you end up jeopardizing your marriage.

What if, at some point in your marriage you really don't feel like you're getting enough sex? First, talk to God about it. Bring it before the Lord. Then nicely talk to your wife. Not arguing. Not accusing. Just asking her to help you in this area of need. And try not to pick bedtime to talk about it if you don't want an argument. Be careful not to come across as critical or judgmental. If you really feel you need more, be honest with her so you protect your relationship.

> Not having enough intimacy—and failing to change
> that—only leads to more problems.

I worked for my dad for over twenty years in a large building with a flat roof. After brutal winters, it wasn't unusual to find we had some leaks in the roof when the spring rains rolled in. The trick was finding the leak so we could patch it. A soggy ceiling tile wasn't necessarily directly below the problem on the roof.

I'd check the steel beams overhead with a flashlight and often found the water was coming in someplace else, far from the wet ceiling tile. Why? Because after the water enters through some kind of crack or hole in the roof, it can travel along steel beams for quite a distance before dripping onto the ceiling tile. I could inspect the roof above that wet ceiling tile all day and not find anything to patch.

The same thing happens in marriage. When a man doesn't feel like he is getting enough sex, it's like a leak in his roof. The situation brews in his mind, and often it will affect him in other ways, at other places in the marriage. He may not seem as attentive or ready to listen. He may be crabby or short with his wife. He may seem inconsiderate in some way. Distant. The symptoms can be all over the place. Some women try to treat the symptoms and never discover the real problem. If this is happening to you, find a good time to lovingly talk to your wife about it. Frequency is important.

Have an established bedtime for your kids when they're young. Get them to bed early enough to give you time to switch gears and love your mate.

When the kids are older, they may be going to bed at the same time you are—or later. You still need to carve out time for just the two of you. Kiss them goodnight and close your bedroom door. The kids knew when our door was closed, we were talking—or something. They had no problem with that. And neither did we.

I have a reputation in the family as being a "lock checker." I check to make sure every door is locked and bolted. Sometimes I forget and I've already climbed into bed and hate to get up—but I do it anyway. I've taken a lot of ribbing about that, but it is a habit I've developed out of a deep desire to protect the family.

Having good, regular, loving sex is marital "lock checking." It keeps each of you safe from intruders who would break in and steal something the two of you share together—your relationship, your testimony, your ministry, and your kids. It keeps you safe from the enemy who would like to ignite some smoldering resentment between the two of you.

This is serious stuff—and good reason to be a "lock checker" when it comes to making time to reconnect and secure your love for each other with regular, loving, unselfish sex.

Remember, like a radio, when you get the frequency right you'll avoid a lot of static and have good, clear, beautiful music instead. I'm a music lover at heart, and that's my wish for you and your wife as well.

Keep Your Guard Up

There are great movies that I've watched once but may not watch again. They have some common, tragic elements to them. A nice guy just doing his job or trying to do a good or heroic thing gets killed because he let his guard down a bit.

Gabriel in *The Patriot*.

William Wallace in *Braveheart*.

Way too many characters in *Saving Private Ryan*.

Often tragedy follows carelessness—or a little mistake in judgment. A moment of trust or confidence when they should have listened to the voice of doubt and reason inside them.

Unfortunately, real life isn't far off from that. "Good" men and women get taken out all the time. A relaxing of their guard. A bad decision. A bit of compromise—and sometimes a whole lot of grief follows. Often this involves some kind of sexual sin. The consequences can be absolutely tragic, and it happens way too often.

When you got married you may have thought something like this: *I did it. I made it. I remained sexually pure until marriage. I won't have to fight sexual temptations anymore.*

Keeping yourself pure until marriage is good, right, and the way it should be—but that's only part of the journey. Now you need to stay pure for another fifty years or so. The battle for purity isn't *nearly* over— because you still have a sex drive. You need to stay faithful to your wife and to God for a whole lot longer than you have so far.

Ideally, being able to have sex as a man and wife should be enough. But there's still potential for danger. Once you've enjoyed sex, your appetite for it increases. So you'll always be vulnerable. When it comes to staying pure, there are plenty of danger zones. My hope, of course, is that you guard yourself well.

★ ★ ★

Keeping yourself pure until marriage is good, right, and the way it should be—but that's only part of the journey. Now you need to stay pure for another fifty years or so.

★ ★ ★

If you want to guard your marriage and your family, here are some things you can do.

Know What the Word Says About Sexual Sin and Traps

Read Proverbs 2, 5, 6, 7, 9, and 23 and underline the verses that talk about sexual sin and wayward women. You'll be amazed at how plain God makes it. The warnings couldn't be any clearer.

God is trying to tell us something here. He wants to make sure we get it. Proverbs, the book of wisdom, warns about women who have sex outside of marriage—how their house leads to death—and how many mighty men they've destroyed. They'll rob you of everything you value and leave you with deep regrets.

Steer Clear

Don't go near her house, as Proverbs advises, or bring her to yours in the form of a movie, cable, or website. Be absolutely diligent about it. The devil is patient and is willing to wait. Hoping you'll lower your guard.

When our kids were growing up, we didn't have the Internet at home. Sometimes school papers required us to take our kids to the library computers. We chose not to have cable either, even though our antenna reception is lousy. My wife and I previewed movies to make sure we didn't inadvertently expose our sons to something that might arouse curiosity to see more.

Was it inconvenient to have a home without Internet access? Definitely. Would some consider these drastic moves? Yes. Will kids be excited about these moves? Hardly. But they turned out to be good ones.

I remember my middle son came home from a high school Bible study one night and thanked us for keeping the Internet out of our home. He talked about how the guys in the study confessed to porn addictions. That they wanted to break free, but couldn't.

If you can't live without the Internet at home, get some heavy-duty filters. But remember, filters aren't foolproof, and there's always the chance that something can get through. With that in mind, keep the computer in a high traffic, high visibility spot. A computer with Internet access in a teenager's room is dangerous.

Smartphones are another issue. I remember the tortured look on a 16-year-old boy's face when he talked to me about his problem with porn. He accessed the porn through his smartphone. I can see why parents want phones for their kids. It's a great safety tool, especially when the kids are out. But buying a smartphone with Internet access for a teenager? Not so smart.

The Bible tells us to steer clear, to avoid every form of evil—and this is a no-brainer. Sometimes you have to go out of your way to stay protected. It may be inconvenient, but it is the safe way—and totally worth it.

Never Let Down Your Guard Around the Opposite Sex

Sexual sin is a killer of good men, women, marriages, and families. Keep your guard up in this area. Don't cut yourself any slack. A little compromise usually ends up in a lot more gushing out. It can whet your appetite, opening you up for more temptation. Don't imagine the Bible allows you any exceptions to the warnings about sexual sin and its devastating consequences.

As a man, there are some women I deliberately avoid. Even Christians. I take special precautions to stay clear of them. They have a questionable reputation, and frankly, I don't want any hint of suspicion going my way. I'd rather err on the safe side.

There are so many good things you want for your marriage and your family, right? Well, sexual sin has the power to dismantle everything. *Everything.*

As a Couple, Don't Neglect Your Sex Life Together

If I go to a grocery store hungry, I'll likely put a lot more things in the cart than I need. If I'm filled up, I'm probably going to walk right by food that would catch my eye if I were hungry. The same principle applies to sex. If you're on a starvation diet, you'll likely be more vulnerable to temptation.

Refuse to Take Matters into Your Own Hands

Here's a topic that doesn't come up often, but let's talk about masturbation a moment. My advice is simple. Avoid it. It doesn't lead to the two of you being closer as a couple in any way. A man was made to need a woman. This drive is part of what pushed him toward marriage—and the commitment that goes along with it. In marriage, it keeps a couple aware of their need for each other.

Typically a man wants sex more than a woman. A wise woman makes sure to satisfy her man—even if she doesn't need it as much or as often as he does. But a man has a responsibility too. Sometimes you just have to exercise self- and Spirit control for your own safety and the good of your marriage. Masturbation fosters fantasy. How can that be helpful to your marriage? Masturbation is all about instant gratification. And instant gratification is the enemy of self-control, which is essential in the battle to stay sexually pure.

Generally couples who are mad at each other aren't about to have sex together. A man may react with the attitude of "I don't need her." If he engages in masturbation he will widen the chasm between them even farther. On the contrary, when a man relies solely on his wife to satisfy him, sex can be a factor to help bring and keep a couple together.

Pray It Forward

One more thing when it comes to protecting yourself and your marriage from sexual sin. Pray about it.

Here's how I handled the matter. I realized we have a free will, which means I could fall. I could choose to sin by having an affair. I understood that God, allowing me to have my free will, may not stop me—and that would be disastrous. If I did something like that, I would definitely not be seeing things clearly, either by choice or stupidity.

So here is how I've used prayer to protect me against such a mistake. I've prayed something like this. "Lord, I am of a clear mind at this moment. I am asking you, of my free will, to honor my prayer. I am asking you to keep me from ever cheating on my wife. I give you permission to stop me, even if at some point in the future I am not thinking clearly and rebelling against you. Stop me. Break my legs if you have to, but I ask that you spare my life. Just don't let me fall in that way."

Now, I don't put God to the test on this. But he has honored my prayer. He has spared my wife and me a world of heartache, deception, grief, and regret known by so many others. I've repeated the prayer to God a number of times. I'd certainly recommend praying a similar prayer yourself.

Sexual sin is something to be very, very aware of. It has nailed some of the greatest men of all time.

It trapped the man after God's own heart…David.

It took down the wisest man of God who ever lived…Solomon.

It destroyed the most powerful man who ever lived…Samson.

No man should discount the danger of sexual sin or get sloppy guarding against it.

I started this chapter by talking about some movies I'll likely never watch again. I'm going to end this chapter by mentioning a scene from one of them, *Saving Private Ryan*.

The movie depicts a string of tragedies and the loss of many good men. I remember one scene as the men storm the beach. A soldier got hit in the helmet by enemy gunfire. The bullet left a nasty dent—but the man was unharmed. He pulled off his helmet and looked at it in disbelief and amazement. Instantly the enemy sharpshooter fired again. The soldier took a fatal bullet in the forehead.

You may feel you've dodged a bullet when it comes to staying sexually pure. That's great. But don't take off your helmet. Don't let down your guard. The battle isn't over—and may intensify soon.

✦ ✦ ✦

A Million-Dollar Marriage

You don't have to be rich to have a million-dollar marriage. Imagine I'm holding two $1 bills. Let's say they represent the typical Christian man and woman getting married. But married Christians can't live like singles anymore. There must be changes.

They can't put their own needs first.

They can't spend themselves however they want.

Now imagine I exchange the two singles for a $2 bill. The two shall become one, right?

When you look at the back of a $2 bill you'll see a picture of the signing of the Declaration of Independence. We forget how dangerous this was for these men. Signing was an act of treason or war—and there was no turning back. To fail would cost them everything. In the same way, when we marry, it's a no-turning-back commitment that will cost us and our kids dearly if we fail. We're no longer singles. We're to be inseparable.

We've already talked about a number of things that show up in Christian marriages, but shouldn't. Here's a partial list of the type of stuff that marks a marriage that is still made up of two $1 bills.

- Arguing, fighting, getting even, being crabby or irritable.
- Punishing each other with coldness, silence, or withholding sex.
- Complaining about or being critical of each other.
- Verbally abusing each other, putting each other down.
- Dredging up the other's past failures and rubbing their nose in it.

- Selfishness—one or both having an "it's all about me" attitude.

- Manipulating each other to get your way or to change your mate.

- Cheating on each other in some way.

- Failing to treat each other as God's special child and gift to each other.

- Allowing the passion to cool, failing to work hard to keep marriage fresh.

- Failing to show appreciation to each other regularly.

- Being impatient with each other.

- Being quick to point out each other's faults and flaws.

- Being disrespectful and rude to each other.

- Loving your mate as long as your mate shows love back.

- Only being willing to meet each other halfway.

Meeting each other halfway isn't a biblical principle, by the way. The "halfway principle" leads to conflict. Men, do you want to love like Christ loved? A man is to lay down his life for his wife if needed. You can't lay it half down. Jesus went all the way to the cross—not halfway.

We could go on. The type of stuff listed above is far too common—even in Christian marriages. This is a vicious cycle. You don't think your wife treats you as she should—so you return the favor. The kinds of things listed above are not part of God's plan for marriage. Most are clear violations of Scripture. Sin.

Sometimes we have the rattiest clothes that we wear around the house. We get used to them. And sometimes we get that sloppy, that casual, that relaxed with how we follow God's Word at home, too. If we want to consistently follow God's plan for marriage—and enjoy the benefits of it—we need to stay on guard.

A marriage like a $2 bill is different. Let's look at some things that belong in a marriage according to God's plan.

- Treasuring each other as God's gift, as God's child.
- Encouraging each other.
- Putting the needs of your spouse above your own needs.
- Being quick to forgive.
- Overlooking faults rather than putting them under the microscope.
- Being patient with each other.
- Being kind to each other—even in the way we talk to each other. Not rude, sarcastic, or short. Not belittling and critical. But genuinely nice.
- Having satisfying and frequent sex.
- Being faithful to each other.
- Sacrificing for each other.
- Consistently working to make the marriage better and keep it fresh and passionate.
- Listening to each other—trying to understand each other.
- Striving to please each other.
- By your actions and attitudes showing there's nobody you'd rather be with than your spouse.
- Treating your mate with love and respect even when they're crabby or aren't showing that kind of love to you.

A marriage like this is priceless. A man striving for a marriage like a $2 bill recognizes his accountability to God for how he treats his wife. He is trying to help and encourage his wife to become all God intended her to be.

And this will do more for your kids than you can possibly imagine. They'll see Christianity in action. You won't have to ask your kids' youth pastor to explain why it's so important to date a Christian. Your kids will *see* the benefits because they'll see how you treat your wife.

It's rare to see a $2 bill in circulation these days, but you can still get them at the bank. I have one in my pocket with my credit cards. I have another one tucked in the edge of a framed picture of Cheryl on my desk. I keep these $2 bills around as visual reminders of the kind of marriage I want. Inseparable. Rare. And so totally worth everything I put in it.

I have no doubt that a multimillionaire would pay a million bucks for a marriage like this, but a great marriage can't be bought. And it won't naturally just "happen." A great marriage is built. And it is built according to God's specs. A $2 bill marriage is certainly worth a million bucks and more. And we can have a great one if we put in the effort.

So how about it? Take a couple singles to the bank and exchange them for a $2 bill. And ask God to help you take your marriage there. Anybody can have a $2 bill marriage, a million-dollar marriage, if they do it God's way.

Frankenstein, Dracula, and the Curse of the Wolfman

This is a monster chapter. Huge. But it's about a monster issue—pornography. This isn't a comfortable topic. It's hard to face, but we must. Pornography is destroying Christians at every level. It is likely affecting you—or someone close to you.

The Frankenstein Factor

In 1931 the great-granddaddy of horror films raised goose bumps on the arms of terrified moviegoers across the United States. In the Hollywood version of *Frankenstein*, Dr. Frankenstein became obsessed with life and death. Specifically the idea of creating life. The doctor and his helper dug up bodies from the graveyard immediately after the mourners left.

With the use of body parts from a variety of corpses, Dr. Frankenstein stitched together his creation. Using the power of an electric storm and a bunch of whiz-bang gadgetry, he brought the "monster" to life. The monster eventually turned on his master and everyone else, wreaking havoc and disaster. Dr. Frankenstein couldn't control the monster; it had a life of its own.

Now, the movie is old. The sets are obvious, the script is predictable, the special effects are primitive, and the acting is the worst of all. It really isn't scary anymore, not by today's standards.

But the real terror factor of this movie is found in a chilling parallel to the Christian life. Its true horror is in the way it mirrors the life of many, many Christians.

As a kid you were probably afraid of monsters in the dark. Your mom or dad likely tried to help you over your fears. "There are no such things as monsters," they said. And eventually you grew up believing what they told you was true.

But it *isn't* true. Not anymore. Monsters *do* exist—and pornography is one of them.

Pornography's cold fingers have pried open the doors of the church. It has a rigor mortis death grip on men and boys who sit in the pews. It has reached epidemic proportions with devastating effects on men, their marriages, and their kids. Succumbing to pornography can crumble your marriage, your kids' respect for you, and everything you value as a Christian.

I once heard someone say, "Most of you wouldn't consider taking illegal drugs. You wouldn't risk the artificial high. You know the dangers—how it will destroy your life. Pornography is the drug of this generation."

★ ★ ★

Pornography's cold fingers have pried open the doors of the church.

★ ★ ★

If you aren't involved in pornography in any way and never have been—great. Excellent. But somebody close to you is. You need this information to understand what they're into and to help them get out. And you need to understand some things about pornography if you're going to go to the drastic measures you'll likely need to protect your kids.

The perspective of someone into pornography will likely fit into one of three categories.

1. "It isn't wrong or dangerous. It's no big deal. It's not like I'm committing adultery."

2. "Okay, I know it's wrong—and a problem for some. But I can handle it. I'm not ready to say goodbye to it yet—but I can if I want."

3. "I know it's bad. I know what it can do. But I can't get away from it. I hate myself for it. I make promises. But eventually I always come back. And part of me is afraid I'll never be free."

In this chapter we'll help those in categories one and two understand what they're into, and we'll help men from all three mind-sets break free.

Dr. Frankenstein was brilliant and talented, yet things went tragically wrong for him. Where did he make his mistake? Where did it start?

Obviously the problem started with wrong desires in his heart, but then he made the mistake of going where he didn't belong—to the graveyard. He dug up things in the place of the dead. He secretly spent time with these dead things, stitching them together. Against the advice of others, against all moral codes, he proceeded with his experiments and brought the compilation of corpses to life.

This is exactly what's happening to Christians involved in pornography. *They're going where they don't belong.* Deep down, they know it. That's why they view it in secret—when nobody is looking.

How "in control" did Dr. Frankenstein feel when his creation came to life? Completely. He felt like he was totally in charge. It is the same with many Christian men, boys—and even some women and girls. They honestly believe they're in control.

They believe they can look at pornography with no ill effects.

They believe they can stop anytime they want to.

But what happened to Dr. Frankenstein? He learned he couldn't control the monster. It was stronger than him. Dr. Frankenstein tried chaining the monster in a dungeon, but it broke free. It couldn't be contained. And it unleashed terror, death, and destruction wherever it went.

Dr. Frankenstein thought he was the master of the monster, but the monster soon became the master.

This is a picture of what happens to Christians who become involved in pornography. Sexual sin can't stay locked up and hidden away. It can't be controlled. It is a monster. It has a way of escaping and destroying marriages and families.

But Jesus conquered sin's power over us.

> We know that our old self was crucified with him so that the body ruled by sin might be done away with, that we should no longer be slaves to sin—because anyone who has died has been set free from sin…The death he died, he died to sin once for all; but the life he lives, he lives to God. In the same way, count yourselves dead to sin but alive to God in Christ Jesus. Therefore do not let sin reign in your mortal body so that you obey its evil desires. Do not offer any part of yourself to sin as an instrument of wickedness, but rather offer yourselves to God as those who have been brought from death to life; and offer every part of yourself to him as an instrument of righteousness. For sin shall no longer be your master…Don't you know that when you offer yourselves to someone as obedient slaves, you are slaves of the one you obey—whether you are slaves to sin, which leads to death, or to obedience, which leads to righteousness? (Romans 6:6-7,10-14,16).

According to these verses there was a time when sin was our master and we were the slave. Sin was in control. And our life was destined for sin's penalties. Death.

But Jesus defeated death on the cross and offered us eternal life as a free gift. And when we became believers, sin's power over us died as well. Sin was no longer our master.

Is it possible to revert back to sin being the master in some area of our life? The verses above seem to back that up—which is really a scary thought.

Like Dr. Frankenstein, if we go back to the graveyard—if we go where we shouldn't go, if we dig up things we shouldn't—then, like Dr. Frankenstein, we will develop an obsession. We're empowering and recharging sin, like the electrodes on Frankenstein's monster. If we bring dead sin back to life, it becomes a monster…and can become master.

And if sin is master, can we stop anytime we want to, like many men tell themselves they can? No. It's not quite that simple.

Ecclesiastes 8:8 says it this way:

> As no one is discharged in time of war, so wickedness will
> not release those who practice it.

Pornography is the kind of sin we're to be dead to. But like Dr. Frankenstein, if we poke around in the graveyard, the place where dead things are, we can bring this sin to life. A gruesome, horrible resurrection of death itself. But often Christians don't see it as a real problem. For most the monster is breathing with a life of its own long before they realize it.

I beg you to hear me. If you are not involved in pornography in any way, never have been, good. *Stay away.* Don't go there.

But if you've dabbled in it or are involved now, even if it isn't frequent, you're likely in very real danger. The very fact that it isn't every day makes you *think* you're in control. And that's the fatal miscalculation. There's no escaping sin and its consequences. Like a cancer, unless you get rid of it, the thing will grow.

Don't think I'm overstating it. I'm understating. I can't possibly convey with mere words the dangers of pornography. I've seen the haunted look in the faces of young men and boys who have tried to break free—and came to the ghastly realization that the grip was too strong. I've heard the desperation in the voices of men who found that pornography had become their master. I've felt absolute waves of chills washing up and down my spine as men shared the price they've paid because of pornography.

Some weep. Others whisper as if all their strength and power is gone. Others speak with the vacant, hollow stare of one who has lost all hope. I've listened, shaking, as they share stories of the carnage in their life from serving this demonic master. The regrets. Despair. Loss. Misery. Fear.

Stories of jobs—*gone.*

Marriages—*gone.*

Respect and love from wife and kids—*gone.*

These are true horror stories that should scare any Christian man to the core. Pornography is right out of hell, and when we really understand the danger of it, the truth should scare us enough to make us run from it. Overstating the danger? Hardly.

Men fool themselves in so many ways regarding pornography.

- "I'm not addicted. I can handle this. I'm in control."
- "I can stop whenever I want—and someday I will."
- "I'm not hurting anyone."
- "This is just my little vice, outlet, entertainment."
- "This isn't affecting me."
- "This isn't affecting my marriage or my kids."
- "If my wife was more understanding, if she would give me more or better sex, I wouldn't need this. It's her fault."
- "I deserve this little outlet. I'm entitled to it. I've earned it. It's my little reward."
- "It's not as bad as actually committing adultery."
- "This isn't affecting my relationship with God—I repent, he forgives."

The truth is somewhat different. I wish we could take the time to debunk each of these false arguments. But let me say this.

The price tag for pornography is huge. It's a monster that will become master. It's anything but harmless. It *will* destroy you, and hurt those you love most in this world. Pornography is wrong. It is sin. The Bible is clear about avoiding whores, prostitutes, or adulterous women—and that would include seeing them in person or on a screen or magazine. Jesus made that clear in Matthew 5:28: "But I tell you that anyone who looks at a woman lustfully has already committed adultery with her in his heart."

And catch the passionate warning in Proverbs 7:25-27:

> Do not let your heart turn to her ways or stray into her paths. Many are the victims she has brought down; her slain are a mighty throng. Her house is a highway to the grave, leading down to the chambers of death.

Are you getting this? Do you see what you're dealing with? Pornography isn't harmless or something a person is entitled to. Those involved in pornography are headed for the graveyard, for the house of death. They may think they aren't hurting anyone, but they are destroying *themselves*. They're making an appointment with death.

If you're involved in pornography, you're playing in the graveyard. You've got to get out before the gates are locked and you're doomed. The Bible isn't giving these commands to restrict our fun, but to protect us from things that can hurt and ruin us.

Vampires May Be Trendy, But They'll Suck the Life Out of You

Vampires have hit prime time. In recent years they've become trendy. Fashionable, even—pasty complexion and all. Some girls think they're tragically romantic. Vampires are stars in movies. Books. Oh yeah, they're regular celebrities. Give me a break.

When I was growing up, vampires were evil, scary, blood-sucking monsters that only came out at night. They preyed on those venturing out alone in the dark.

Count Dracula was the creepiest vampire of all. Played by Bela

Lugosi in *Dracula*, the 1931 horror classic, he was nothing like the dreamy vampires cast for movie roles today. Dracula's eyes were pure evil. His smile was enough to turn a victim's blood cold. Which is probably why Dracula wasted no time getting to their neck. He liked his blood warm, thank you very much.

Like Frankenstein's monster, vampires were destructive. Deadly. Too powerful to control. Pornography is like the worst kind of vampire. It will suck your dreams from you, claim your future, and rip away those you love.

Let's look at eight ways pornography can mess up great sex in marriage. Ways it can suck the life out of satisfying sex with your wife. This is important for single men, too. If a single guy is into pornography, he is destroying his potential future for good sex with the girl he'll marry—the love of his life.

1. Pornography gives false expectations. It portrays a false image of what sex is like in marriage. It shows a life of continual sexual gratification. When sex in marriage isn't that frequent or exciting, it will lead to arguments and problems in your marriage—which will totally hurt your sex life.

2. Pornography promotes selfish sex. Sex is about expressing true love. Pornography is about unleashing pure lust. Big difference. It's about *getting*—and is built on greed. In marriage, you'll begin to want your wife to satisfy your desires that are getting more selfish. She'll sense and recognize the lust—and pull back. This will certainly damage your sex life.

3. Pornography masks the tragedies of sex outside of marriage. Pornography portrays sex outside of marriage without the negative consequences. Without crippling regrets, guilt, or the misery of living a lie. It hides the truth that sex outside marriage leads to disease, unplanned pregnancies, loss of jobs, respect, marriages, and families. Your sensitivity to these lies lowers—making you more vulnerable to temptation. Unfaithfulness in any form will hurt your chances of good sex in marriage.

4. Pornography twists your tastes. Married guys who get into pornography often will prefer imaginary sex to the real thing. Men will give up the chance for sex with their wife to indulge in the fantasy world of pornography. They find it more exciting, more stimulating. It offers an empty, counterfeit sense of intimacy without requiring a man to be a responsible, decent man and husband. Sneaking off to view pornography, masturbating, and preferring that to sex with your mate is twisted, and will gut your dreams of a great sex life in marriage. And without frequent, healthy sex with your mate, something between you will die.

5. Pornography will push you to live out unhealthy fantasies. Guys into pornography need more and more to satisfy them. Eventually they'll look for other ways to fulfill their sexual fantasies. None of those paths lead to anything good. This is deadly—lethal—to a guy whether he's married or not. And it will implode a good sex life with your wife.

6. Pornography fosters a spirit of resentment toward your wife. You start thinking not about how wrong what you're doing is, but about how wrong your wife is. *If she would just be a little more interested in sex, like some of the women in the pornography, I wouldn't need this stuff,* you think. Suddenly you're the victim. Instead of being her protector and addressing the real problems, little by little you actually distance yourself from her.

7. Pornography is addictive—whether you're married or not. Unmarried guys tell themselves that they'll drop pornography after they're married. The truth is if you're into it before marriage, you'll likely still be involved in it after you're married. And the way brains develop, the younger a guy is when he looks at pornography, the tighter the grip of addiction. If a woman feels her husband is addicted to porn, what do you think that will do for their sex life together?

8. Pornography will poison your wife, your relationship with her, and her ability to give you great sex. If you're into pornography even occasionally, your wife may see that as you being unfaithful to her. Pornography becomes the other woman. Here are three kinds of things that will go through her mind.

I can never satisfy him. I can never be enough. She'll feel she can't compete—and she doesn't want to. She sees a prostitute as not being faithful to a man and likely loaded with STDs. She sees them as tragic, broken women on a path to spiritual, emotional, and physical death. The idea of having sex with you only reminds her of the prostitutes you're viewing. It'll make her want to avoid sex with you. She'll want to avoid anything she thinks the prostitutes are doing because she doesn't want to be like one or be treated like one herself. She'll become more inhibited. Thinking about pornography may rev you up, but it will repulse her. A woman will often divert her love, her energy someplace else. Kids, eating, escapes—or another man.

My body isn't good enough. The fact that you look at other women tells your wife she isn't enough for you. She isn't young enough or attractive enough—things she can't change.

That leads to feelings of defeat, low self-esteem, and a general sense of "Why keep trying?" She will become more self-conscious and inhibited sexually, further widening the chasm between the two of you.

I can never trust him. She'll see you as choosing pornography over her. Because you're looking for sexual thrills outside of marriage, because she sees pornography's power over you, she'll lose trust and respect for you—foundational necessities for a healthy marriage. Her love for you will shrivel and die. What do you think that will do for your sex life with her?

Pornography unravels everything—every tie you have to her. Pornography promises excitement, but robs you of the love and relationship you value most. It's like Frankenstein's monster. Too powerful to control. It's like the vampire, Dracula. It'll suck the life out of your marriage and sex life together.

The longer you put off beating this, the more likely this monster will destroy you. It's time to stop playing in the graveyard. The dead are there, and they have no intention of letting you leave. But you can. You must. And you must do it now.

Let's look at how to break free.

The Curse of the Wolfman

We've looked at Frankenstein and Dracula. And now the third of the big three horror film monsters…the Wolfman.

The 1941 Hollywood story of *The Wolf Man* as portrayed by Lon Chaney Jr. tells of Larry Talbot, a decent man who is bitten by a werewolf. The wound heals, but Larry doesn't. The bite cursed him to the terrifying future of becoming a werewolf himself. At first Larry denies it. His rational mind rejects the thought that anything has changed inside him. He believes he's the same man he always was. But when the moon is full this man is transformed into a vicious, powerful beast that kills innocent people. When he realizes the truth, it scares him to the core of his being.

Larry is tortured with deep remorse and hates the monster he's become. He desperately searches for a way to be free, but nothing can change him back to the man he once was. His resolve is strong, but the pull of the night and the beast within prove stronger.

In the end, Larry is convinced that the only way he'll be free of the monster is death itself.

There's a parallel to the man who's been exposed to pornography. Like Larry's encounter with the werewolf, a man can brush the whole thing off. Sweep it under the rug. Bury it. In his rational mind, he dismisses concerns about pornography infecting him. Changing him. Taking control.

But pornography is a monster. Like a werewolf sinking its fangs into a man, the man *is* changed, whether or not he realizes it. The lust for more is in his blood, and time after time he feeds the appetite for pornography. He may stay away for a period of time but eventually gets pulled back in, just like the Wolfman succumbed to his primal urges with every full moon.

The man bitten by pornography sees how it hurts himself and those he loves. He finds that no amount of self-loathing seems to change the vicious cycle he's caught in. No personal resolutions or acts of self-control can keep the powerful lust, now working deep within him, at bay for long. He always goes back to pornography.

The man bitten by pornography becomes a wolfman himself. I see them at conferences frequently. Their stories are all a little different, yet always the same. They are desperate men. Tortured. Feeling cursed. Doomed. Men unable to break free from the monsters they've become. Men who fear they'll never know freedom until after death.

But there's hope. I've talked to many men who have found true freedom—and are forever grateful.

My wife's grandpa, Art Hansen, worked for Al Capone. Art was a young man at the time. He told me how he had a pack of "dogs," as he called them—henchmen he would sic on anybody who didn't do things "Big Al's" way.

Art Hansen was a tough man. He told me it made no difference to him whether he beat up a man or a woman. He felt no remorse. He worked for a monster—and had become one himself.

But he met a girl, Alice, who eventually became my wife's grandma. Alice was a preacher's daughter, but Art asked her out anyway. She wouldn't date him, but invited him to church. In time, Art got saved. He saw his need for God's forgiveness, for a new start in life. He recognized his need for a new master…not Al Capone anymore, but God himself.

God changed his heart. Art knew he had to get out of the "racket," but he never knew anyone who got out alive. Anybody who left the organization was a potential threat to Capone. He might talk. And Art had seen firsthand what happened to others who talked too much. He had a friend like that in the organization—someone who hadn't kept his mouth shut. One day while Art and his gangster friend were riding a Chicago streetcar, a black sedan pulled up alongside and someone inside gunned down the one with loose lips. One moment they were talking—the next moment Art's friend was dead.

So when Art Hansen went to the boss to tell him he'd been saved and couldn't do that kind of work anymore, he expected the worst.

He promised to keep his mouth shut—but he also knew they had a way of making sure he did. As it turned out, God worked in the gangsters' hearts to give him a chance.

They showed up regularly—guys Art recognized as Capone's men. They let themselves be seen so Art wouldn't forget to keep quiet—and so he'd remember they still knew where to find him.

But he got out and grew to be a godly man. Strong—but gentle. He told me once that God took his heart of stone and turned it into putty.

Art Hansen was freed from a powerful monster by God's grace. That same God is at work today, freeing people from monsters within.

There is hope for you as well. You can be free from this monster of pornography. The curse can be broken. With true repentance, a strong desire to change, faith in God, self-control, and the help of the Holy Spirit, God can help a man be free from this curse.

Let's look at ten starting points for breaking free.

1. Confess and repent to God.

You've probably done this many times. But do it again now. And anytime you fall.

Make a heartfelt confession. Admit you're wrong. This is not your wife's fault or anyone else's. You chose to look at pornography. We fall to temptation because we've fostered wrong desires. We have to accept that responsibility and blame.

Heartfelt repentance means a desire to turn to a right behavior. This is about expressing your desire to change direction—and backing it up with action.

2. Understand yourself. Why do you keep turning to pornography?

If you understand what drives you to pornography, it may help you know how to combat it. Often a guy turns to pornography for one of several reasons. Is it curiosity? Lust? An escape? Revenge against your wife? Whatever it is, it's time to move on. Don't use it as an excuse. Fight to be free.

3. Spirit control...a Christian's source of supernatural power.

We looked at this in chapter 3. Without the Holy Spirit, you'll be "white-knuckling" your way through this, likely with little real success. You'll be like Larry Talbot, the original Wolfman, unable to "will" yourself to change with self-control alone. Spirit control is absolutely essential.

Ask the Holy Spirit to change your desires and your heart. He doesn't force himself on us. We give permission, by our free will, for the Holy Spirit to work. Ask him to help you break free. Recognize and acknowledge your inability to do it on your own.

Our whole culture works against deliverance in this area. Advertisements and media work from the conviction that sex sells products. Our culture embraces it. So realize you'll need to ask the Holy Spirit *daily* to continue to help you and change you.

Deliverance may not happen instantly. I have never heard a man tell me he had instant deliverance from pornography. It may be a long, hard struggle. One reason? So you don't ever forget the struggle. So you don't ever go back. A long struggle often strengthens a man. You need to keep giving it to him. You need to keep asking him to change your desires.

Exercise faith in our almighty God. Remember who you're dealing with. *God.* And remember what he's done for you. He's given you a new nature. He's defeated the power of sin and death with Jesus's sacrifice on the cross and resurrection. You need a certain element of faith that God has released the power of sin's grip on your life. You need to reach out and take that truth by faith.

4. Self-control. Exercise willpower.

Yes, we ask God to change us, but we also need to take steps to combat our old nature.

Remember Proverbs 25:28. "Like a city whose walls are broken through is a person who lacks self-control." To protect yourself and those you love, get some walls of protection built. If your repentance is genuine, there should be action you're taking to back that up. Here are three areas to consider.

A. Get rid of triggers. When Jesus talked about dealing with lust in Matthew 5:27-30, he talked about cutting off your right hand if you need to. In other words, attack it ruthlessly. Don't allow pornography an easy bridge back into your life. Remember, you're fighting a monster here. You must destroy it. This isn't about trying to cage it, control it, and make it your pet.

Get rid of your pornographic DVDs, magazines, or whatever. Clean out your computer. Cancel your cable service. Distance yourself from people who are a bad influence. Cancel your Internet service— if that's how you're accessing pornography. You can survive without it. Go to the library to get your e-mail. If you must keep your Internet service, install strong filters. This is especially important if you have kids on the computer. Even if you install filters, remember not to fully rely on them. *You* are the filter. If this self-control and submitting to Holy Spirit control doesn't come from your heart, this isn't going to work.

B. Watch where you go. Stay off paths that lead to temptation. Proverbs 5:8 says, "Keep to a path far from her, do not go near the door of her house." How are you going to do that? There are probably a million ways to access pornography. Where are your vulnerable points? How can you avoid it?

Maybe it's staying up late on the computer. Maybe you face temptation when you travel. Make your hotel reservations at a place that doesn't offer adult movies—or ask the front desk to activate the child controls while you're signing in. And don't just surf the cable channels late at night. You're asking to be tempted. I met a man who insists the hotel remove his TV when he checks in. He told me the hotel does it, or he walks.

C. Don't masturbate. Masturbation isn't exactly the way to build self-control. It generally involves fantasy, which is built on lust. According to Jesus in Matthew 5:27-30, that's sin. Masturbation reinforces instant gratification, not self-control—which works against you in the fight against pornography. The only sexual release a married man should have is with his wife.

5. Accountability.

Keeping this thing totally secret—in the dark—isn't the best idea to conquer it. You need to get your problem with pornography out in the light. If you decide to be accountable to another man, be sure the accountability has some teeth to it. Pick a guy who cares enough to be tough on you.

6. Talk to your wife.

This is tricky for me to make this part of a blanket statement—as if this fits for every person in every situation. Ask the Lord to help you with this as far as when to do it. In most cases I believe you *need* to confess this to her. Not just to shed a sense of guilt, but because you didn't keep your wedding vows. You weren't really faithful to her alone. Your wife is your soul mate. In my opinion, you need to talk to her about this. This will involve asking for her forgiveness and help. Be careful not to blame her or heap guilt on her. This was *your* choice.

She'll likely have a hard time understanding why you do this. She may get very mad. You know it certainly will hurt her—which may be part of what helps fuel you to beat this. Regardless, she needs to understand what you are doing to help yourself. Tell her the steps you are taking and the things you're trying to eliminate. This is critical. Your confession will probably rock her world. She needs to know you *do* want to be free and that you're working on it. That you have a plan.

Finally, she needs to understand how she can help. Give her permission to ask you regularly, "How are you doing?" But don't get all defensive with your response. "I can't believe you're asking me that. Don't you trust me?" She wants to trust you, and asking you is part of building it. Commit to always tell her the truth, even if you messed up. Which should be a *really* good incentive to keep you from messing up. I think a good wife would be the ultimate accountability partner.

7. Strengthen your love.

If you're married and involved in pornography, you've compromised when it comes to truly loving your wife "above all others." Recognize that. Confess that to God. Ask him to help restore your love for her. A strong love for your wife will help you fight for her and will ultimately help you defeat pornography's grip in your life.

8. Keep yourself in the Word. Get in it daily.

This is your source of truth in a world of lies. This will help you see things in black and white. The Bible is a source of strength. You'll learn to love and fear God more—both of which will give you strength in the fight. And obviously you'll need to put what the Word says into practice. "How can a young person stay on the path of purity? By living according to your word" (Psalm 119:9).

9. Don't give up—keep fighting.

Always stay on guard. It's like a remodeling project. Sometimes the mess gets bigger before you get to enjoy the new room. And as you attack pornography's grip, as you try to tear it out of your house, expect things will be hard there too. If you stumble, get back up and keep going. I've never heard a man say it's easy, but it is critical to your survival.

Remember who and what you're fighting for. Yourself, your marriage, your kids, and your relationship with the Lord. "Be on your guard; stand firm in the faith; be courageous; be strong. Do everything in love" (1 Corinthians 16:13-14).

For some it will be an ongoing battle that grows easier in time. Don't give up.

10. Get professional help.

There are times a man's tie to pornography involves more than disobedience. More than bad choices they've made. It may be linked to other things—maybe from childhood. For some it involved some kind of abuse.

For whatever reason, if you need a counselor, get one.

Restoring a Normal Sex Life

When your wife learns of your involvement in pornography, she won't exactly be eager to jump in the sack with you. Which can make matters worse if you're not careful. Here are some things to remember.

Be patient with her. Give her a chance to sort things out in her mind without putting huge sexual expectations on her. Go slowly.

Work on strengthening your marriage and her respect for you. Consistently do the things you should be doing as a husband according to God's design. This will help heal her self-confidence, which probably took a major hit when she learned of your involvement in porn. It will also begin to rebuild her respect for you. This will make it easier for her to accept you and your love.

Rebuild trust. It will take time. Lots of time. You can't demand trust once it has been broken. Keep doing the right things, even though it is hard. Show her love, even if she isn't returning it.

Work toward making sex a priority between you again. When the time is right, talk to your wife about both of you making intimacy more of a priority in your marriage. You'll need this in your fight against pornography's grip in your life, and to restore your marriage. Talk to her humbly and with love. Ask your wife what she needs—how you can do your part to make more intimacy a reality. And when she tells you something, don't take offense to it. Take notes.

Don't wear your glasses to bed. Sometimes a guy who is into porn no longer finds his wife's body arousing. He's focusing on outward beauty. Ask God to help you love her from your heart. As you stay away from pornography, the attraction will follow.

Show some gratitude. After you've had sex, tell her how much you appreciate her. Hold her. Show her how grateful you really are.

Don't think living without pornography will be miserable. This is really important. I've talked with guys who are torn. They want to get away from pornography, but they want to have it, too. They can't imagine living without it. But that is a bit of the addiction talking. When they get free from the monster's grip their vision and perspective seem to change.

The testimony I hear over and over from men who have fought free, with God's help, is one of great joy in living God's way. At one time they were torn, too. They wanted pornography and hated it at the same time. But on the other side of freedom they want nothing to do with pornography. The shame is gone. They see things differently. More clearly. They are grateful men who never want to go back.

Men, there is hope, but there's also a ticking clock. You need to get out *now*. God forgives and God can change you, but consequences are still an issue. Your involvement in pornography is dangerous for you, your marriage, your wife, and your kids.

I've talked to guys at conferences who were free from pornography's grip, but it took losing their marriage to wake them up. And along with their marriage, they lost the respect of their kids. Don't let that happen to you. Fix this before you lose those you love most in this world. This is high-stakes stuff.

Guys, I'm pleading with you here to guard yourselves, and your wife and kids in the process. Don't let sin be your master, controlling your thinking, actions, and choices.

Don't be like Dr. Frankenstein, going to the graveyard where he didn't belong. Digging up the dead and creating a monster. We're dead to sin, and dead things are best left buried. Don't be playing in the graveyard. The dead are there. "Whoever strays from the path of prudence comes to rest in the company of the dead" (Proverbs 21:16).

Don't let pornography, like the vampire Count Dracula, suck the dreams and life right out of you. Don't let it steal the potential for great sex with your wife.

Don't stay under the curse of the Wolfman. In a way, Larry Talbot was right. The only release for a werewolf is in death. And Jesus died to kill sin and its power. The Bible tells us we need to die to ourselves and live in the power of the Holy Spirit instead. We can be free.

* * *

Don't Wait for Hallmark

When someone goes on a job interview, one of the things they're interested in is how many days off the company provides. Sick days, personal days, paid holidays, vacation days. Everybody likes days off.

We've talked about the importance of treating your wife special. Creating your own holidays is one more way you can do that. Sure, you already have Christmas, Valentine's Day, your anniversary, and birthdays. But the more special days you can celebrate, the more fun you'll have. You might add the anniversary of the day you started dating—or got engaged.

Men, you don't have to spend lots of money, but you'll really make her feel loved and secure if you remember special days—and put effort into keeping them special. Homemade cards are perfect. I make plenty of cards for Cheryl—and they're no less special than store-bought ones. Just the opposite.

I've heard guys gripe about the "Hallmark Holidays." They refuse to participate. They talk like it's nothing but a marketing gimmick to separate them from their money. They're actually proud about the fact that they don't get suckered in by all the nonsense. They may be right, and it may be a fine attitude for a guy to have *as long as his wife feels the same way.*

And that's the key. Men, how does your wife feel about it? Somehow I can't imagine them bragging to other women they know, "Your husband got you a card? What a loser. My husband is a real man. You'll never catch him getting a card or some silly little gift to say he loves me."

You don't have to buy a card—but do *something.* Women *want* to be remembered. To feel special. To know that some of those key dates in your history together are valued by you—because they all led to the two of you being together.

My folks used to declare "unbirthdays." Any random date would do. It was an excuse to go and celebrate. To have ice cream or make a routine day really special. Cheryl and I celebrate a number of holidays every year besides the usual ones. March 8—our wedding anniversary. March 24—the day we got engaged. December 7—the date we officially started dating. We average at least one "holiday" a month.

Early in our marriage Cheryl and I started "You're Something Special" days. We didn't spend money, or if we did, it was very little. It wasn't about presents, but the gift of time spent with the other person. It was about showing we cared enough about each other to plan ahead and make each other's day a little brighter. For me, it was a way to show Cheryl how special she was to me.

As time went on and kids started coming, this tradition turned into "You're Something Special *Week*." It was something just between Cheryl and me. It's about planning little things to give each other—like the time I made the boys' school lunches for a week. It might include doing things together that were outside our normal routine. That gives us something to anticipate and look forward to. It adds spice to a relationship.

And add holidays throughout the year. Maybe you're facing hard times. Maybe your wife is just not feeling life is all that much fun. So initiate an impromptu holiday to give yourselves an emotional lift. Change the routine. Go out for ice cream. Do something fun. Expand this for the whole family. Kids will really enjoy this break of routine, too.

Men, imagine interviewing for a new job and being told you can create your own holidays. *Paid* holidays. And as many as you want. They'd have people lining up for that position.

In reality, that's not such a ridiculous scenario. See, as a husband and dad, you're the head of a brand-new entity. And it is entirely within your authority to declare some holidays. Not that you'll be ducking out on other responsibilities, but you don't let those responsibilities grind you into a rut. Sounds good, doesn't it?

So get your calendar and circle some dates. The Hallmark ones for sure. Then add some of your own. It's like giving your family a mini-vacation. You'll be glad you did. Put some of the stress of daily life behind you, even if just for a day. Help your mate and your kids enjoy the simple pleasures of life. Take a vacation from your problems, and you'll all be better equipped to handle them when the holiday is over.

Good Things Come in Dozens

Sometimes things that come in dozens are a welcome sight. For women? Roses. For men? Donuts. And this chapter is going to cover a dozen things you can do to strengthen your marriage and keep it strong. Actually, make that a "Baker's Dozen"—because we'll cover thirteen things. As you see something you should work on, circle it or highlight it.

And you might want to fold over the corner of this page right now. This is the kind of chapter you'll benefit more and more from as you review it. You ready? Okay, let's go.

1. If you've gotten sloppy, confess it to God. Ask him to open your eyes and change you.

By this point in the book I'm sure you've seen ways you can improve. Things you've let slide. Areas where you've gotten sloppy.

Start by confessing this to God and then to your wife. But don't stop there. Confession should be accompanied by repentance—a sincere heart to change direction backed up with action and deliberate effort. God can help with that, too, if you ask him. Remember the principles of self-control and Holy Spirit control. You're going to need that to live the way the Bible teaches us to live.

2. Love your wife according to God's principles for love. That's your goal.

Take 1 Corinthians 13 literally…and the verses shared from Song of Songs back in chapter 1. Get rid of the things that typify hard hearts and $1 bill marriages, and cling to the things that make up $2 bill marriages. We looked at a whole list of those things on page 103.

3. Lead with love.

Leading is not a license for a man to push a woman around verbally, physically, or with his "authority" as husband. Those are bully tactics. That's wrong on a man's part. Broken. Abusive.

We're to put our mate's best interests at heart. We never saw Jesus lead with intimidation—and that's not how he leads the church. He led people with love, and he gained their undying devotion, respect, and love. If we're going to love our wife as the Bible tells us to—just as Christ loved the church—we probably need to make some changes in how we lead.

Before you make a decision, be sure you've really considered her feelings and opinion on the issue. And hey, when you make a mistake, admit it. Good leaders do that. Apologizing should be a regular thing—when you mess up, 'fess up.

Lead with God's principles for love. That's your goal.

Maybe you're thinking, "She wasn't this way when I married her." Okay. Maybe that's what being married to you did to her. Sometimes the greater the change you feel she needs to make, the greater the indicator that there are changes needed in you. As the leader, you're responsible, to a certain extent, for the kind of woman your wife becomes. When I see wives who appear lazy, selfish, complaining, bitter, or unforgiving, I know somewhere their husband failed with part of his leadership responsibility.

4. Know your mate's primary love language—and show her love that way.

The five love languages were articulated by Dr. Gary Chapman.* While people often identify with a combination of these languages,

---

* Dr. Gary Chapman, *The 5 Love Languages* (Chicago: Northfield Publishing, 1992).

most people have a method that expresses love to them best. Here are the main ways people prefer love shown to them.

- *Acts of service.* Giving them a hand. Getting a job done for them.
- *Physical touch.* Holding hands. Hugging. Sex.
- *Gifts.* Things given to show your love.
- *Quality time.* Just being together. Listening to each other.
- *Words of affirmation.* Encouragement. Verbal expressions of admiration, respect, love, and support.

If you don't know what best expresses love to your mate, ask. This is important. If the best way to show love to your wife is by spending quality time together, don't expect staying late at the office will do it. Even if you think you're showing love by providing for the family, she'll interpret it an entirely different way.

This is critical for your kids as well. Know their love language and speak it.

5. Don't try to fix all the things that are wrong with your wife. Work on yourself first.

Has the Lord nudged you about changing something? What's your wife been asking you to change? Is there a habit or something you do that annoys her? Talk to her. Ask her if you don't know. Find out if you're missing something. "What can I do to be a better husband?" Don't argue, criticize, defend yourself, or go silent. Often those are manipulating tactics. If you do something like that, she may not open up to you in the future—and then you'll be flying blind.

And if your wife asks what she can do to be better for you, be tactful. Kind. Humble. Gentle. Respectful. Speak the truth in love. And if you have a list of things you'd like her to change, pick *one.* "Here's number one on my wish list." Give your wife too much to work on and she'll likely get discouraged and never really start.

6. Don't be afraid to confront, but be careful how you do it.

Sometimes you need to confront your mate. But do it tactfully. Be wise, like Esther and Abigail as we talked about earlier in the book. Be mindful of her ego. Your goal must be to bring out the best in your wife, not to win an argument or prove a point.

7. Listen to your wife.

God often refines us through our mate. God has used Cheryl to help me change in so many ways. We're cutting ourselves short if we don't *really* listen when our mate shares her heart with us.

So listen. Repeat things back to make sure you understand. Then work on it and ask for her feedback. That's hero stuff. Don't let your pride get in the way.

8. Work on your marriage daily.

We're task-oriented. We make our little "to-do" lists. But you need to add one thing to your daily list. "How can I show my love to her today?"

- *Think about your spouse during the day.* Think about what you want to tell her and things you want to do with her. You did this all the time when you were dating, didn't you? Find little ways to show your wife you're thinking about her. Sometimes a quick text message will be the brightest spot in her day.

- *Put on your best phone voice.* When you see her name come up on your phone, answer it like you're really glad to talk to her—like you used to do when you were dating. I often hear men on their phone being rude, harsh, and loud. I know they're not talking to their boss or to a client. They're trashing their wife about something. That's stupid and wrong. That's hurting yourself. You want her to know you're always accessible—no matter how busy you are.

- *Show some excitement.* When you see each other at home

after work, let her know you're happy to see her. Smile. Kiss her. Hug her like that's the best part of your day—like you want to see her—and not just for sex.

- *Talk nice.* Don't get sloppy at home. Sarcastic, rude, cutting remarks and criticism all work to quench passion in marriage. Be kind. Considerate. Work on this—it makes a huge difference.

- *Tell your wife what you love about her regularly.* Things that make you proud of her. Things you appreciate. Remember the things men tend to take for granted—the things she routinely does that you don't even think about anymore.

- *Be interested in her life.* Ask about her day. Her concerns. Her work, worries, and fears.

- *Show you truly value her.* One great way to do this is to seek her opinion and input on things. This says "I value you—and your opinion." This says "I think you're smart."

- *Practice what was preached.* Take your Christianity seriously. Did you get an elbow in the ribs during a sermon? Did the Holy Spirit nudge you? Take the hint—and put what you're learning from the Bible into practice. Don't make excuses for not following God's Word.

- *Have some fun together.* When you were dating, you looked forward to the times you could be together. You didn't just sit in front of the TV when you were with each other. You'd go out, do fun things. Are you still doing that? Go out and get some ice cream together. *Do* something. Life gets routine. Put something fun on the calendar that you'll both look forward to.

9. Don't give up, even if she doesn't seem to notice.

Do the right thing, whether or not it seems to make a difference. That's going to take some self-control. That's going to take some real control by the Holy Spirit. Don't expect your mate to make immediate changes, but the more you work on being the husband you should be, the more likely she'll notice—and start making changes herself.

Watch for any steps in the right direction on her part—and encourage them. If her attempt at improving isn't noticed by you, she may give up and go back to old ways. Show appreciation in her love language.

10. Go on regular dates.

I try to take my wife on a date every week. It's so good—I really hate to miss one. This is a time to talk. Listen. Dream. Reconnect.

- *You need to initiate the dates.* If you leave it to her, it won't have the same impact—and you aren't leading.

- *Plan it out.* Put a little thought into it. You don't have to do something exotic and totally unique every week, but have a plan. This shows your wife that spending time with her is important to you. That's money in the bank.

- *Dates don't have to be expensive.* Ours are usually at a fast-food place. You'll develop favorite date spots. That's good. The key is to be together.

- *If you can't afford to go out to eat, just go out.* Someplace. Anyplace the two of you can walk and talk.

- *Dress the way she'd like you to dress.*

- *Hold her hand while you drive or walk to the restaurant.* Show affection—publicly.

- *Be a gentleman.* Open doors for her. Help her on with her coat. Common courtesy goes a long way.

- *Turn off the phone.* If you're worried about kids, have a special ringtone for them, or commit to only answer the phone if it is the kids or the babysitter. You want to communicate that there is nobody you'd rather be talking to than your mate. A date should be a time to disengage with everyone else—except your wife.

- *The Internet can wait.* Resist the urge to check the Internet for anything during a date. It saps your attention. You'll be looking at a screen instead of your mate's eyes. And once you're on the Internet, it's hard to pull away. I've seen so much of this—and it sends a really bad message to the one you're with. Can you imagine someone going out, and their date pulls out a newspaper? Or they pull out their mail and start opening letters? Totally rude, right? That's exactly what you're doing if you get online while on a date. You're checking the news and opening mail.

- *Pick a chick flick.* If the date involves a movie, make it one she'll enjoy. And if it's a chick flick, don't complain. That isn't manly. Men will fish, hunt, and camp in all kinds of rough conditions without any complaining. Why? Because they're men. They can take it. Think of a chick flick the same way. Be a man. Don't complain or make fun of the movie. Consider this. If my wife watches some romantic movie she'll probably be in a romantic mood afterward. That works for me. On the other hand, if I pick some action movie, she'll likely get motion sickness. I learned this the hard way. So watch the movie of her choice, with your arm around her or holding her hand. Does she cry watching movies? If so, have some tissue in your pocket to hand to her. It shows you know her and that you care.

- *Save some good news for date night.* Something interesting at least. I actually make a little list of things to talk about. Have you ever seen those couples sitting in some restaurant—not saying a word to each other? They're sitting at the same table but living in different worlds. That's a zombie date. I pray I never end up like that—and I work at it so I don't. You don't want a zombie date either. So bring things to talk about. Even if it's current events or some crazy story. During the week, if you get something you'd like to tell your wife, don't be so quick to waste it on a

quick text message to her. Jot it down and save it for the
date if you can.

- *The date is to be an oasis.* An escape. Don't use it to beat her
down with criticism. This is a time to encourage and build
up. Don't use a date to bring up projects you want her to
do for you. This isn't a business meeting. Dates should be
fun. Make it enjoyable.

- *Look in her eyes when you're talking.* Is she happy? As the
leader, you need to realize that's part of what the date is all
about. You're maintaining your marriage, and you want to
make sure your wife is doing okay. When I owned a one-
hour photo lab, I could tell if the machine was running
right just by the way it sounded. If it wasn't, I worked on it
until I found and fixed the problem. Everything depended
on that machine running right. The same thing applies to
your wife. Can you tell if she's had a hard day just by the
tone of her voice? Sure you can. Watch her body language.
Her eyes. Do you see love? If not—you'd better work on
that.

- *Get to know your wife—and help her know you.* We all
change. Are you keeping up with your mate? Do you know
where she's at? Who she really is? Who she wants to be?
Find out how your wife is changing…it may surprise you.
And *help your mate know how you're changing.* Too many
times a couple's life is completely wrapped up with the kids
and their activities. When the kids leave, they find they
have nothing left in common. Don't let that happen.

- *Every once in a while have a "State of the Union" date.* The
sole purpose—understood by both in advance—is to
evaluate how each of you feels the marriage is going. But
you've got to be open. Your wife may have some things
that are bothering her that you'd rather not hear. As hard
as it is, you need to listen or she'll eventually bury it…or

worse yet, confide in someone else. Try not to get defensive about it. Sure, sometimes you can explain things, but if you can't take a little criticism you won't get a lot of honesty. Then work *hard* to make noticeable changes.

You can do this, guys. You *need* to do this. Date your wife—and use it to strengthen your marriage.

11. Get the physical thing going.

Have sex. Have it more often. Be creative. If you want to stoke the fires of passion and strengthen your marriage, this is foundational.

Go to bed at the same time. If one of you has to get up early, fine. But go to bed at the same time. If you don't, it's pretty hard to be intimate. And sex is pretty important to a strong, passionate marriage. You may not feel tired—or may be in the middle of a project when your wife wants to hit the sack. But make a commitment to go to bed together and stick with it.

And going to bed at the same time isn't only about sex. It's about taking time to connect after a day apart. A time to talk. Our culture, work habits, schedules—so many things work toward pulling a man and wife in different directions. You must fight that—especially when it comes to going to bed together. Remember one of the big reasons you got married in the first place. You wanted to be *together*. Don't let that slip away. When it comes to bedtime, synchronize your watches.

12. Step up to be the spiritual leader.

This is a biggie. Most Christian women would love their husband to be more of a spiritual leader in the home. Many find it *attractive*. And the more your wife sees you take the lead spiritually, the more she'll respect you and trust your judgment. There should be a class for guys getting married that clues them in to exactly how to do this. But here are a few ways you can get the spiritual leadership thing going in your home.

Get into the Word daily. You can do this. And it will change you over time. Before skipping to the next point, think about this for a moment.

If you're not in the Word daily, I have one question. *Why?* You're a *man*. It's time to man-up and do the right thing. *Make* the time. I'm up early to get in the Word. If I don't do it before my day hits the treadmill, I'll have a lot harder time getting to it. You say you're too busy to get into the Word? Or you don't think you really need it daily? Doesn't that sound just a bit arrogant?

Apply the things you learn in God's Word. Otherwise, what's the point? Imagine looking down and noticing your zipper is open. You'd fix it immediately, right? The only thing dumber than standing with your zipper open is not fixing it once you *do* see it. The things you hear in a sermon or read in the Word are important and you need to put them into practice—pronto.

Talk to her about something you read in the Bible. A verse, principle, or story and what it means to you. This would be a good thing for a date. Your wife will probably love it—and it's incredibly easy. You can do this.

Teach the kids spiritual truth. About God and the principles he's given us to live by. Some call this having family devotions. It's a key way to step up to be the spiritual leader your wife longs for.

Pray together as husband and wife. Be real and vulnerable—admitting struggles and asking forgiveness in prayer. It doesn't have to be every night. But do it sometimes.

Let me share a little secret with you about understanding women. We all know it can be a little tricky understanding what is on their mind at times, right? Pray with her—and listen when it's her turn to pray. You'll learn plenty. You'll get insight on where she's at, what her concerns are, and what's important to her. Then, as the husband, as the leader, you've picked up some great intel on how to better meet her needs and help her where she's at. This *works*.

Keep working to grow spiritually. Learn at church, from other men, from books, and your own Bible study. You must keep growing or you'll get stagnant. Remember, deep down your wife wants you to be a godly man. So if you stop working at it, you're stunting yourself, your relationship with God, *and* your marriage.

Don't settle for going through the motions on Sunday. Driving to church can become a tense, argument-filled time. There's stress getting everyone ready and out of the house. Often that means you're running late. Yelling or giving abrupt orders. As the man, you can fix that. You can get up earlier and find ways to help more to keep things running smooth. That sure beats the image the kids will have otherwise.

Show it's important to learn about God. Bring your Bible to church. Bring a notebook and take notes. Everybody knows people don't remember nearly as much when they only listen as compared to when they listen *and* take notes. Your kids know that. And your kids know *you* know that. So if you don't take notes, what's the message you're sending? "I know I won't remember as much, but I'm okay with that. This isn't that important to me."

Show it's important to honor God. By setting aside tithes and offerings without your wife needing to remind you. And when it's time to sing, belt it out. Put some enthusiasm into it, regardless of your voice.

13. Keep your mate as your number one.

Cheryl and I loved our kids like crazy, but our kids knew Cheryl was my number one. And they knew I was her number one. This is critical. Essential. Marriages get in trouble when they put the kids first. I'm not suggesting you neglect your kids. Not at all. But there needs to be a clear message given.

Sometimes this means you'll need to prioritize things a bit. Maybe you need to limit the sports your kids are involved in if you're running ragged getting them to events to the point where you have little energy left for each other. I know of one couple who just never had time for sex because they were so busy with the kids. The wife thought her husband should be more understanding. She felt he needed to get his priorities straight. He thought he needed a divorce—and that's what he did.

And our bed was for us. My wife and I. Not the kids. Sure, a bad dream or a storm might be an exception, but there is danger to allowing kids into your bed regularly.

In the long run, you're not doing the kids any favors if you put them above your mate. Be sure you and your wife talk about this.

We hit thirteen things here. Areas you can work on to muscle up your marriage. Some of these are going to take a little sweat, but the payoff is undeniable. If you do it God's way, your wife can help you so much—and bring you such happiness. And the example you'll give your kids is pure gold.

Work on these things and your marriage will improve in dozens of ways. You can do this—with God's help. Live according to God's principles, even when it doesn't seem your wife is responding to it. That's hero stuff. It's the kind of thing most men miss. Be a hero, men.

What Are You Aiming At?

Imagine you're driving a minivan with all your kids inside—and me. You're idling at the edge of a massive mall parking lot, which is totally empty. I ask you to pick out a parking spot a hundred yards away and park there. You'd have no problem easing that minivan right between the painted lines, right?

But what if we repeated the whole thing with you blindfolded? To make it more interesting, I grab the wheel and have you turning circles for a full minute. Think you'll find that parking slot? You'd probably wrap your minivan around a light pole instead.

The key to hitting a target is aiming. Unless we keep our eye on the target, our aim will be off.

The same principle applies when parenting kids. What are you aiming at? We'd love the things on this short list below to describe our kids—especially after they're grown.

- That they'll have good character and integrity.
- That they'll have a good attitude and perspective and relate well to others.
- That they'll avoid pride, complaining, and arguing.
- That they'll live in a way that makes a difference in this world.
- Ultimately, that they'll love God and serve him wholeheartedly.

We want these things for our kids, but unless we aim at that, unless we take deliberate steps to help them get there, we're shooting blind. We'll likely miss the mark.

Our culture is toxic. The morals and worldview our kids pick up from movies, TV, music, peers, and more can work like a slow poison. By the time the effects are obvious, the damage is deep. Our culture often teaches our kids that what we as Christians believe is good is really *bad*, and what we believe is bad is actually *good*.

As parents, we need to take deliberate aim to help combat the effects of those influences in our kids' lives. There are many ways we do that as parents.

The most important one we've already talked about throughout the first part of this book. Consistently living right yourself. Not letting down your guard and getting sloppy with your Christianity at home. It's about being the Christian man the Bible says we should be, whether we feel like it or not. This is critical. If you don't get that part right, understand you'll severely diminish your ability to influence your kids for real good.

Next, teach your kids about God and the principles he's given us to live by. You help kids learn to tie their shoes, wash their hands before they eat, and with countless other things—right? In the same way you'll teach them about God in formal and informal ways. Leaving this to the church isn't enough. As a man, you need to step up and teach your kids as well—for their own protection.

I've written books on this topic, and each one is packed with practical ways you can hold kids'—and even teens'—attention while conveying a nugget of truth.

- Blowing up eggs in the microwave.
- Smashing tomatoes.
- Messing with glow sticks, mashed potatoes, and paintball guns.
- Crazy outings in the car, to the grocery store, and at a used car lot.

All of these little activities, and plenty more, are highly effective ways to teach kids critical spiritual truth. Who says teaching our kids has to be boring—or hard? Check out these books. It's easier—and way more fun than you can imagine.

If we want our kids to go in the right direction, there are things to do as parents that are just plain smart. Things to avoid. Others to embrace. Ways to encourage good influences on your kids and limit the bad. We'll go over these in upcoming chapters as well.

There are a bazillion good books floating around on parenting. Psychologists, doctors, pastors, and plenty of other highly qualified people have written all kinds of important things about behavioral and developmental issues. So I won't be going there with this book. There are other things I need to tell you about. Things we've found to be important or critical in raising kids. The types of things you may not be reading in other books. That's where I'm going to focus.

We need to talk about where you're aiming. Because when it comes to raising your kids you need to keep your eyes on the important things. To help you sort that out a bit, I'm going to make a statement below—and I want you to decide if you agree with it or not. I believe it with all my heart. The question is, do you?

> As our kids grow up, they won't be truly happy unless they learn to genuinely walk with the Lord—regardless of how good they do in school, sports, music, or drama.

Do you agree with that? I'm hoping your answer is *yes*. Good. Now let's take it a step further. As parents we've been entrusted to raise our kids to responsible adulthood. So imagine your kids are grown now. Here's another statement—one I fully believe. How about you?

> Our kids won't be truly happy no matter how good a job they land or how much money they make if their relationship with the Lord isn't real and relevant in their lives.

Do you agree with that? I'm guessing you do. Great. Now, in light of these two statements *that you totally agree with*, I need to ask you the big question.

What are you aiming at? Where are you focusing your efforts?

In years of working with youth and in church leadership, here's what I often see: Christian parents emphasize education, sports, drama, or music. That's it.

Not that there's anything wrong with these, but they aren't enough. They're not the most important issues in life. We've already established that when you agreed to those two statements above. Your kids need the spiritual aspect. Deep down, you *know* that's the most important thing.

If all we truly emphasize with our kids are their education and extra-curricular activities, we're fooling ourselves. What makes us any different from any other decent family that doesn't have anything to do with Christ? *Not much.* Why should we be surprised if our kids grow up without Christ being their priority?

Sure, we go to church on Sundays. But if we aren't emphasizing spiritual things to our kids throughout the week, doesn't God seem like an add-on to our week? An afterthought? Certainly our kids wouldn't get the impression that he should be the most important part of our lives.

Let's take a quick look at some of these areas Christian parents tend to emphasize—often more than their kids' spiritual walk.

Education

This is the biggie. There's nothing wrong with education. It's a really, really good thing. Important? Absolutely. But is it the *key* thing in life? No. The key priority with our kids is their spiritual walk. If education were the answer, our culture would be in a much different place.

Our world is filled with well-educated people who are going to hell—and leading a parade of others there. There are many, many well-educated people making really foolish choices in light of eternity. Education is good, important, and needed. But it's not number one.

We need to be careful what message we convey to our kids. Often, the way kids see it, education is the priority.

"Do you have any homework?"

"Is your homework done?"

"We need to get those grades up."

Kids aren't seeing the same intensity when it comes to spiritual things. We're quick to make sure kids are keeping their grades up, but seldom check to see how they're doing spiritually. We check to make sure the homework gets done—even help our kids do it—but rarely make sure they're having daily time in God's Word. We make every effort to be sure kids don't miss a day of school, but missing church occasionally is no big deal. We push for the chance to enroll kids in advanced classes, but there isn't the same eagerness to help them understand deeper spiritual truth.

No wonder kids grow up thinking education holds the answers for life. No wonder they think they need a good education so they can get a good job that pays decent money—so they can be happy. Without realizing it, that's exactly what their Christian parents taught them.

Sports

Okay, I know I'm walking on sacred turf here, but think about this with me for a moment. Sure, kids can learn all kinds of great things from sports. Perseverance. Patience. Self-control. Caring for others. Humility.

Gee, sounds like we ought to dump going to church and just sign the kids up for more sports. Which is almost what happens in some Christian families.

You can learn great things from sports. But when you make sports the schedule priority over church, you're stepping out of bounds. I know men who had their kids highly involved in sports. It wasn't just Sundays that took a hit. It was much more. Their kids missed a lot of youth group events—and as a result, they never felt plugged in. They were at practice instead. After practice, they had to do homework. Consequently, their closest friendships developed at school. And when they got older, they really had no interest in church. By the time kids go to college, they've picked up a subtle and dangerous message about what is important in life. Many drift from the faith. Surprise, surprise.

When our kids were young, we didn't sign them up for all kinds of sports. With two of our boys, basketball was their preferred organized sport. We signed up in a neighboring park district that didn't play games on Sundays. It meant a little more travel time, but we guarded Sundays.

> ★ ★ ★
>
> When you make sports the schedule priority over church, you're stepping out of bounds.
>
> ★ ★ ★

My wife and I made sure they got to church youth group events after practice. It was more work—but keeping them involved at church was that important. That's where our kids developed their deeper friendships.

We were also careful of avoiding back-to-back sports. We didn't want the kids spending more time with their coaches than they did with their dad. And our kids did fine with it. As a dad, I played with the kids when I got home from work. And since they weren't always at a practice, they often had their homework done by the time I got home. Now *we* were free to play.

We played baseball, basketball, street hockey, and football. In the summer we swam, snorkeled, and water-skied. We also just messed around. Had fun. Chasing each other. Play fighting. We made up our own games. I spent endless hours playing "jail tag" with my boys and their friends. They loved it. And I formed a critical bond with them. Why would I want to just send them off to practice every day?

Yes, the kids can learn humility, self-control, sportsmanship, and all kinds of other things from organized sports. But they can learn them better from Dad. As I spent more time with the kids, it also allowed me to tie in spiritual truth. And when we went to church, it didn't mess with their game or practice schedule.

I'm not against organized sports. But I also know they can pull kids out of the orbit of church and spiritual things. I'm not saying sports is to blame or that sports are evil. But I am saying that pursuing sports, over the long run, can be a game that results in few wins and many injuries—in a spiritual sense. Sometimes it's us, the dads, who want our kids in sports. It can be a heady thing, especially if our kids have athletic ability. It's ironic that sometimes sports can lure our kids away from the Lord while we sit in the stands and cheer.

So be very careful in this area. Know the limitations and subtle dangers.

Maybe you feel an aggressive sports life is the best plan for your kids. It worked for you. Hey, I respect that. Just realize you'll need to work extra hard to get your kids plugged in and comfortable with friends at church—especially as they hit the critical junior high and high school years. Remember, the kids they spend the most time with are the ones they'll feel most comfortable around—and the ones who will influence them most.

How will your kids handle less involvement in organized sports? Better than you think, if you're doing the dad thing right. If you're spending time with the kids, you'll probably find they don't miss organized sports as much as you thought they would. Often *parents* have the harder time giving up the sports. Sometimes parents push sports because *they* love it so much. I loved going to games, and hated to see that era end. But I never regretted the extra time I got with them— or instilling the importance and priority of church in their lives.

Music, drama, or other activities

There are tons of things we can get our kids involved in. Great things. But always look at the long-term effects. If it will busy them to the point that attending church will be hit-and-miss, think long and hard about it.

> ★ ★ ★
>
> Kids can learn humility, self-control, sportsmanship, and all kinds of other things from organized sports. But they can learn them better from you.
>
> ★ ★ ★

If it squeezes your schedule too tight dashing them off to practices, think about the negative effect it may have on you. Your marriage. Your ability to make your spouse number one. Your energy level to be there for her—and hers to be there for you.

But we're supposed to make sacrifices for our kids, right? Sure. But sacrificing time with your mate isn't your sacrifice to make. Sacrifice your time with e-mail? Yes. Sacrifice time on Facebook or other social networking? I'm giving you a standing ovation.

But sacrifice the strength of your marriage? Bad move. Everybody loses eventually, including the kids.

Sometimes the biggest problem parents have is limiting the extracurricular activities their kids get involved in. Pick one or two a year. Don't try to hit something every season. Make life a circus and you'll play the clown.

The job of a dad can be summed up this way:

- He provides.

- He protects.

- He prepares kids for the future.

- And he does all of this from a heart of love.

The things I'm talking about in this chapter—looking out for our kids' spiritual well-being—hit every aspect of being a good dad. It's all about providing, protecting, and preparing. Don't miss this.

I took my youngest son camping on an island in the middle of the Mississippi River. Long after dark we sat on the beach poking the campfire and watching barges navigate the black waters.

I separated one small chunk of flaming wood from the fire and set it on the sand. Handing Luke a squirt gun, I asked him to try to extinguish it. He quickly had it smoldering.

We put the smoking wood back on the campfire and watched it reignite. Then I asked Luke to try to put the fire out while the stick was still part of the campfire. He emptied the squirt gun into the flames, but this time the water seemed ineffective. It turned to steam almost immediately. The campfire blazed as strong as ever.

Now it was time to tie in some spiritual truth, and I'll tell you what I wanted him to learn. The campfire is a picture of the church—which is simply made up of a lot of individual Christians burning in their devotion to God. Like the logs on the fire, as long as the Christians are together, they tend to burn bright for God. They aren't vulnerable. But when they're away from the group they're an easy target. Much easier to extinguish.

And so it is with our kids.

When we're involved in church, attending regularly, and bringing our kids, too, we're protecting them in many ways. We get strengthened, reignited. And so do our kids. When we're away from church we're more susceptible to things that can cool our devotion to God.

Take a look at these familiar verses.

> Let us hold unswervingly to the hope we profess, for he who promised is faithful. And let us consider how we may spur one another on toward love and good deeds, not giving up meeting together, as some are in the habit of doing, but encouraging one another—and all the more as you see the Day approaching (Hebrews 10:23-25).

We're to encourage other Christians to love others. To do the right things. Often, we do this when we go to church. Which is another reason the Word says that we aren't to get lax in our church attendance. Today many have redefined "regular" church attendance to mean going every other week or so. Yet Hebrews 10:25 warns that the closer we come to the end, the *more* we should be attending church and encouraging each other—not less. This isn't exactly a popular viewpoint in our busy culture. But if we ignore God's teaching on this issue, how can we expect great results? What are we aiming at?

Some are in the habit of attending church when they can. It is convenience-based—not conviction-based. They're missing the love and encouragement they might have had—or given. They're missing chances to reignite their faith, their passion for God. And the scary thing is—their kids are missing out as well.

Sometimes attending church is the first thing to go when a family gets busy and needs some "family" time. They have time for sports, social networking, and so many other things during the week. But going to church to worship, learn, serve, and encourage others doesn't rank quite as high.

That sounds dangerous to me. I think you want to make a real effort to be in church every week. Your kids won't feel part of the group if they aren't there enough. And they won't be as connected to leaders and other role models who can help them stay on track.

We took a different route. We wanted our kids to be involved in the club programs offered at church during the week. It was essential for strong friendships. And the things we were trying to teach them at home were reinforced at church by leaders and others. Different voices, same message. That's important.

When I was sick, I stayed home, but Cheryl went to church with the kids. And I did the same if she was sick. If one of the kids wasn't feeling well, my wife or I stayed back, but the rest went to church. It's important to show your kids the priority of going to church. And not just to "get," but to give to others.

When you've been in a church long enough you begin to see how beautifully it all works. Kids that I led as a high school leader when I first got married were my kids' leaders as they grew up. Now my kids are leaders in the youth programs ministering to their former leader's kids—and the cycle keeps going.

Getting to church can be tough at different stages of parenthood. But it's a choice. A commitment. And for us, it's just what we did. Cheryl made sacrifices to get the kids to Awana and youth programs when they were young. She found ways to make it fun, even with Chicago traffic. And it worked—really well.

Be really, really careful about switching churches when you've got kids in sixth grade and older—because it has the potential to really mess them up. Rip them from some established friendships, force them into a situation where they're the new kid—and you might get trouble. Some kids never reconnect at the new church.

That's a big risk, and for what? Better preaching? A shorter drive? A better worship band? At this stage of life you shouldn't need to be church-hopping to be sure you're fed. You should be able to do that on your own during the week.

If you feel you need to change churches at this critical point in their lives, be sure the move is about reaching, protecting, and providing better for your kids. Help them see why you're making the decision—and ideally have them involved in it.

Church has been a haven for my family and me—especially when we've gone through tough times. We've found strength and encouragement—and helped others in the same way. We've developed our best friendships there. Had many of our deepest spiritual moments there. Church is where we've gained rich rewards from serving. That's where I met Cheryl, the love of my life. And where both of our married sons found their mates.

We started this chapter talking about parking your minivan in a specific parking spot at a large mall—and how hard it would be to do blindfolded. Remember, as a parent you've been entrusted with the job of raising your kids to love God and serve him with a whole heart. You have a very specific target to hit. Don't let anyone blindfold you or get you sidetracked. There are plenty of good things your kids can be involved in, but you need to choose carefully. You need to be sure you're not so busy with a lot of good things that you never get time for the best.

What are you aiming at? If your kids won't be truly happy in life unless they have a solid relationship with God, be sure that's the message you're really sending them.

★ ★ ★

Pulling Out in Traffic

Pulling out into traffic can be tricky. You have to be all there. No distractions. You keep your hands on the wheel and your eyes on the road looking for a break—an opportunity to merge safely.

Talking about spiritual things with your kids is a little like pulling into traffic. You need to watch for opportunities, and sometimes create them.

When you see a clear opening, take it.

I'd planned a camping trip with my boys at the Indiana dunes area along Lake Michigan. As I drove down Interstate 90 with my youngest son, Luke, who was about seventeen at the time, we passed billboard after billboard advertising "gentlemen's clubs." I kept my eyes on the road, not wanting Luke to think I was looking at the signs. I glanced over at him. He was robotically staring at the stripes on the road too.

It dawned on me that he'd seen the signs, too. I mean, he was seventeen—and the billboards were the size of semitrailers. He was doing the same thing I was doing. He didn't want me to think *he* was looking at the billboards.

Instead of avoiding the subject, it was a perfect time to talk about it. "I hate those signs," I said.

"Yeah," Luke said, still staring at the pavement. "Me too."

"They're traps. Trying to sucker men to pull off the highway. Men who probably have a wife and kids."

It was an opportunity for a little impromptu spiritual teaching about avoiding traps. It was a good talk.

You want to grab those moments when they come up. I'm not talking about blasting kids with some kind of rant on a topic. But if you can get a nugget of truth in conversationally…that's really good.

Don't avoid the tough stuff.

When you're going through tough times, it's an excellent chance to show them how you're processing things. How you're trusting God. Or maybe how you're using God's Word to get you through. You'll be helping the kids understand you. And in the future, when they're grown and facing hardships themselves, they'll reach back in their memory and remember how you handled things.

We closed a family business when our kids were twenty, seventeen, and fourteen. This wasn't the first time they saw us experience tough sledding. Sharing our fear and faith with them was important at the time—and will help them in their future.

Teach lessons through the news.

There are many, many things you can teach impromptu just by talking over current events or some news story with your kids. Do it. The Word is totally relevant. Help them see that. When you see violence, remind them that God is in control. When you see injustice or corruption, remind them how God is good and just, and that he will settle accounts someday. When you see the results and consequences of someone lacking self-control, remind them of the wisdom of obeying God's Word.

Create your own informal opportunities.

Sometimes there's an issue you want to address. Or you see an article that perfectly illustrates a key life lesson. Print the article and share it with the kids along with the application. Share the name, place, and what happened. You can pick these stories up on reliable Internet news sites. Often they'll have obscure articles about some crazy thing that happened. I've gotten real mileage from these.

Life is busier than a four-lane highway. But look for opportunities to share a timely spiritual truth or an important life lesson in a casual way during the week. And when you see one, don't miss it. Step on the gas and make the most of the teachable moment.

* * *

Superman and Other Heroes

I grew up with Superman. Bought the comic books. Watched the TV series. I have a Superman lunchbox in my office today. The man of steel. Faster than a speeding bullet. More powerful than a locomotive. Able to leap tall buildings in a single bound. Superman was quite the hero.

And when our kids are little, they look at Dad the same way. Like he can do anything. *Anything*. He's Superman. But eventually their viewpoint changes—and that's as it should be. They realize their dad isn't the strongest man in the world. *But he's still their hero*. And that's as it should be, too.

My definition of a Christian hero is pretty simple.

A hero does the right thing and doesn't quit—even when it's hard.

A hero accomplishes the plans God has for him, with God's help.

There's no reason you can't be a hero. Always. For their entire life.

Deep down, *that's exactly what your kids want*. They want you to do the right thing and not quit—even when it's hard. They want you to follow God—accomplish God's plan for your life.

Tough job? Yes.

Doable on your own? Probably not.

Doable with God's help? Absolutely.

The problem is, we tend to get sloppy. Casual with how we live. We compromise. We aren't careful to live like a Christian should at home. And this is one of the biggest problems with parenting—or rather why parents lose their hero status and become ineffective. It gets worse, because often this paves the way for rebellion.

Why Kids Rebel

Some kids simply make bad choices. They know what's right, but they choose the dark side. That's tough. The prodigal son probably fit in that category. I have good Christian friends who've gone through that heartache. One couple, after twenty-five years, saw their son come home to the faith. I don't know if there's a lot a parent can do but wait and pray in some of these cases.

Some parents push their kids toward rebellion—probably without knowing it. In my opinion, this may be the number-one reason kids rebel, but one that seems to stay under the radar. Rarely do parents connect the dots and see this—at least not until it's too late. And it has everything to do with being a hero.

Many parents fear teenage rebellion. They keep a short leash on their kids as they approach the teen years in hopes of heading off the sullen, sarcastic, disrespectful attitude many teens display toward parents.

When disrespect and rebellion begin to show, parents are grieved. Confused. *Where did this come from?* They begin to check who their kids are hanging out with, who their Facebook friends are, and often become convinced all those "bad" friends are the culprits behind the rebellion. There is an element of truth there, but it is only a partial answer.

It only makes sense that if you want to prevent disrespect and rebellion, your first priority is to discover what's driving them in that direction. Friends provide the *vehicle* for rebellion, but generally not the *fuel* that runs it. This is critical to understand. Friends are a factor in the rebellion, absolutely, but they are not the cause as often as we'd like to think. Find the fuel depot. What's fueling the vicious attitude you see?

The motive for rebellion, the fuel for rebellion, is often the parents themselves. Christian parents often look for the culprits among the friends their kids hang with. Parents really need to look in the mirror.

It comes back to the hero thing. Kids want their parents to be heroes. To do the right things and not quit—even when it's hard. To be kind and loving when they come home from work, even when they've had a tough day. To love their mate the way they should—even when they're not loved back. To do the kinds of things we talked about in so many of the earlier chapters of this book. Doing the things the Bible tells us we should do.

Parents tell their kids how God is real and how we should follow him. How he's given us the Bible to show us how to live. They'll even correct their kids and quote Bible verses to show them right from wrong. Christian parents make a really big deal about following God, following Christ, and doing life God's way. So far so good—but all that changes if parents compromise. If they don't live consistently by the same standard themselves, something really bad happens.

The seeds of rebellion are often planted when the child is getting into the "tween" years—nine, ten, eleven, twelve. This is when kids notice disconnects between what parents *say* is important and how they actually live. If parents don't live the Christian life consistently at home, kids can become disillusioned. They lose respect for their parents. Some get angry deep inside. Who can blame them?

Imagine somebody you really look up to. Respect. You'd eventually lose respect for them if they lived by their feelings—by their own set of rules—even though they teach others to live a different way. They'd cease to be your hero.

Our kids can experience the same thing. This erosion of respect for parents often remains hidden. Just below the surface. But it grows. Kids begin forming a fuel depot. By not consistently living out what you told your kids was right and good and important, you're not living like their hero. You're actually destroying their hero—and you wonder why they treat you like their enemy?

A parent who robs their kid of their hero becomes a villain. That makes some kids angry. And when this child gets older, bigger, and stronger, that anger and lack of respect is itching to show itself.

This is the part where friends come in. Other friends who've lost respect for their parents. Often friends provide the courage or the opportunities to lash back at parents. But the *motives* were already there long before the friends provided the *means*.

So what do you do? Yes, be very aware of the friendships they are forming. We'll look at that in the next chapter. But first, be aware of how you're living. Realize the key to curb rebellion is often in your hands. Don't get sloppy and compromise your Christian walk. Hear me on this. What I'm saying is truth—so let this sink in. We're talking about a key to curb teenage rebellion before it has a chance to start. This should be written in twelve-inch flashing neon letters for emphasis. This compromising that Christian parents do is wrong—and tragically costly when it results in your kids losing respect for you. And the price

* * *

A parent who robs their kid of their hero becomes a villain.

* * *

is higher than you might imagine. When your kids lose respect for you, you lose your voice with them. They won't listen. Which means they'll resist your advice. Your warnings. And when that happens, how can you protect them from the dangers all around them?

How you treat your wife can prevent rebellion—or foster it. Look at those earlier chapters where we listed things that do and don't belong in a Christian marriage. Know this: If you talk disrespectfully to your wife, someday your kids will probably do it as well. But if you're careful to respect and treasure her, chances are the kids will, too.

Living right can be hard. True. But that's what heroes do. They do the right thing, even when it's hard. Even when their mate isn't meeting them halfway. This takes Holy Spirit control and self-control.

Kids want you to be a hero. In a healthy way—not on some unreal pedestal. And deep down, *they* want to be a hero someday, too. So when you get sloppy, you're crushing their expectations for the present and affecting their hopes for their own future. If *you* can't be a hero, they may not believe they can, either.

I'm going to make a statement that I fully believe. Read it carefully. Slowly.

It's very hard to rebel against somebody you totally respect.

Think about it. Can you think of somebody you really, really respect? Do you want to please that person? Do you want to put your best foot forward when you're with them? Of course. And so if your kids are rebelling, likely they've lost respect for you for some reason. You need to earn that back. And if your kids are younger—make sure you never lose it.

I'm not talking about demanding respect from them because you're the parent. That approach strengthens motives for *rebellion*, not respect. I'm saying you need to live right—according to God's plan, especially at home, in a way that earns their respect. When you mess up, 'fess up and ask God to change you.

Kids want you to be a hero. To do the right things even when it's hard. Even when you're tired. Even when you're busy. Even when life doesn't seem fair.

And as you do, their respect for you will grow. You'll keep them from building a fuel depot of resentment. You'll keep them from having a motive to rebel.

The only thing that could take Superman down was kryptonite. It weakened him. Made him ineffective. And for you and me, for parents who desire to be heroes, our kryptonite is compromise. We must live the way we know is right whether we feel like it or not. Anything less will weaken us and make us ineffective with our kids.

We'd had a big snow and my sons were messing around outside with their friends. I quickly pulled on a royal blue snowsuit, boots, gloves, and a ski mask. The killer touch? A bright yellow towel for a cape. I know a hero doesn't actually need a cape, but it definitely adds something. "Blue Guy" the *not-so-super*-hero was ready for action. I bounded outside and attacked the kids. They loved it. An hour later I trudged inside. The cape was long gone—pulled off by the kids. I was wet. Tired. And happy.

A couple days later I ran into someone I knew.

"I drove by your house the other day," he said. He gave me a funny look. "Where you running around the yard wearing some kind of blue outfit—and a *cape*?"

"Ah yes. That would be Blue Guy."

He shook his head. "You're crazy."

Sometimes. But I wouldn't have traded that time with the kids in the snow for anything. Kids love having a hero around.

It isn't always easy being a hero. Some may even make fun of you for trying. Many won't understand. But do it. Work at it. Life will be better now, and you'll protect your family's future.

Men, be a hero. The cape is optional, but being a hero is not.

Pushing Their Buttons

Compromise isn't the only way dads erode respect. There's another way it happens. The secret is found in Ephesians 6:4: "Fathers, do not exasperate your children; instead, bring them up in the training and instruction of the Lord."

Exasperating our kids will get them hopping mad—and eventually cause them to lose respect for us. Let's look at nine ways dads push their kids' buttons.

1. The Double Standard. Telling kids to live one way, but not consistently living by the same rules. This has a lot to do with what we talked about earlier in the chapter.

2. The Inconsistent Standard. The rules keep changing, or they're different for every kid. The way we discipline can be a factor here. Imagine playing a game of Monopoly where the banker keeps changing the rules. Frustrating, right? Kids experience the same feelings if we aren't consistent.

3. The Relaxed Standard. It seems you don't care enough to set clear boundaries. Think about that. Boundaries are often set up to keep us safe—so if you don't have clear boundaries, it tells kids you really don't care.

4. The Rigid Standard. The rules or boundaries are too hard. Often kids will think *any* boundary is too tough, so you need to use your head. But be sensitive. Have good reasons for the boundaries you set up. I know people who like to get to bed early. That's smart. But it doesn't work with teens. "I need you home by 9:30—I have to get to bed." Try that and you'll exasperate your teen. You'll need to do a lot more listening—and work at coming up with creative alternatives.

Maybe that means you need to adjust *your* schedule rather than expect them to work around you. Could you take a nap after work so you can stay up later? Probably. Can you move your devotional or workout time to the evenings so you can get up a little later? I'll bet you could. Be flexible—and often you'll avoid exasperating the kids.

5. Lame Explanations. They need to understand the "why" for guidelines or rules. The older kids get, the more important this is. Of course, there are times you just expect them to obey, without explanations. They're learning obedience. But if you help them understand the *why* behind your guidelines, you'll also be teaching them discernment. You'll be helping them consider other factors when making a decision. Smart move. And once they understand your thinking, they will have an easier time being obedient.

On the other hand, if you don't explain, expect them to test the guideline or resent it. Neither of these reactions lead to good places.

Sometimes parents don't *have* good reasons for the guidelines they set up. That's why they resort to giving lame explanations like, "Because I said so" or, "Because I'm the parent." These kinds of responses totally exasperate our kids. Here's the way kids hear it: "Because I'm the dictator. Because I'm selfish. Because I don't care about your concerns."

Set reasonable guidelines, and rethink them as the kids get older to be sure they're still relevant.

6. No Voice. Kids need to be heard—especially if you're disagreeing with them. You may be right. The logic your kid is using may be fuzzy at best. But you need to take time to hear them out. If they don't think you're listening, they'll get exasperated.

What you're communicating to them is that you don't think they've got anything of value to say. If you hear your kids saying things like, "But you don't understand," that's a warning for you. They don't think you're listening. Or they don't think you really care about them. So give them your attention. That means close the lid to your computer and look at them. Their eyes. Their body language. And the dumbest thing you can do is pick up your smartphone while they're talking.

Don't be in a rush. Stick with it until you understand their viewpoint. You may not change your original course of action, but if they really feel you've listened, the intensity of their exasperation won't be as strong.

7. The Game Is Fixed. Kids need to feel like they have a fighting chance—especially when they're disagreeing with you over something. They need to feel you'll actually consider what they're saying. That you'll weigh their logic and change your mind if you agree. If they think your mind is made up and you're just going through the motions of listening to them, you'll fuel their frustration.

If you as the parent always have to be right, always have to win, you'll exasperate them. They'll feel the game is rigged. What's the point of even trying to talk to you or listen to you?

In 1987 Nintendo introduced a game called Mike Tyson's Punch Out! The player went in the ring against a string of boxers. If you beat one guy, another one would follow—and he was bigger. Faster. Tougher. Cheryl and I were high school leaders at our church. One of the guys in our program told me, "Talking to my dad is like playing Mike Tyson's Punch Out. I can never win."

I never forgot that, even after all these years. This dad seemed to feel he was always right—that his perspective was the mature, Christian one. And like a boxer in the ring, he beat his son down with it. His son resented it. He was exasperated. And when he got a little older, he showed it.

As parents, sometimes we're wrong. Sometimes we need to give a little, hear their viewpoint, and apologize. Sometimes we need to come up with a different course of action. And sometimes we have to stick to our guns. But if possible, don't make that decision until you've heard their viewpoint.

8. Easy Target. Kids need to feel safe when they're talking with you. You know where their buttons are, and if you push them just because you can, you'll exasperate them. They're an easy target, and if you resort to belittling or insulting them, you're being a bully. People don't respect bullies. They may fear them, but they definitely don't admire and respect them. That isn't what you want. This fuels anger, rebellion, and sometimes hatred.

9. Wild Card. There are certainly more ways kids feel exasperated with parents. You may do things that exasperate them without knowing it. It may be something you could fix or change fairly easily—if you knew what it was.

So ask them. When things are going well, take them out to a fast-food place. Don't wait until you see them glaring at you from across the room. Ask them some questions. "What are some ways I totally exasperate you? How can I avoid exasperating you when we talk?"

If you want them to hear your criticisms, you'd better listen to theirs. It's hard. And it hurts. But take it like a hero and learn from it.

First Thessalonians 2:11-12 shows how Paul dealt with the Thessalonians as a father deals with his children. It gives us a glimpse into what a good dad should do with his kids. "Encouraging, comforting and urging you to live lives worthy of God, who calls you into his kingdom and glory." Did you get that? Your job is to encourage, comfort, and urge your kids to live a godly life.

Remember, the best way to handle rebellion is to head it off before it starts. You can do that. Don't lose their respect, or if you already have, look at the issues in this chapter so you can rebuild it. Remember, it's hard to rebel against someone you totally respect.

A Haven and a Hangout

Home Is a Haven

Everybody needs a safe zone. A haven. A place where there are no bullies. No bad guys. A place where they're loved. Protected. A place where they can speak without being criticized. Where they can mess up without feeling totally humiliated. A place where they can rest, find peace, gain strength, and get encouragement.

That's what your home is supposed to be for your kids. *Home Sweet Home* isn't just something painted on a plaque as a decoration. It's a reminder of what our homes should really be like. Of what we need to strive for.

Think of some of the creatures you would not want to face out in the wilds. Alone. In the dark. Miles from any help. And without a weapon.

- A 14-foot alligator
- A 650-pound grizzly bear
- A 6-foot diamondback rattler
- A 200-pound carnivorous Komodo dragon
- A rabid gray wolf with a hungry pack behind it

Now imagine somebody breaking into your house at night and letting one of these beasts loose—inside your home. You wake from a deep sleep, but you're not sure what roused you. You sit up, hold your breath, and listen. And then you hear something. The sound is definitely coming from downstairs. You tiptoe across the hall and start down the steps, pausing for a moment to stare into the darkness. Then you see it—*and it sees you.*

All right, that's a creepy example. Dangerous beasts like this don't belong in your home. And here's the point. You need to see any sin as a dangerous beast.

- Bitterness
- Unforgiveness
- Anger
- Insults

- Harsh talk
- Jealousy
- Selfishness

These and so many other things don't belong in a safe Christian home. For the sake of your marriage and for the sake of your kids, you need to get the beasts out of your home—and keep them out.

Your job is to create an atmosphere of love and encouragement. If you're in a bad mood, it'll rub off on others. If you care, encourage, and show love and kindness it will have a positive influence on the whole mood at home. Here are some ideas for ways to do just that.

Make an ice cream run. Sometimes we just need a break—and so does our family. So run out and pick up some ice cream. Some kind of treat will often lighten things up in the house.

Move from ref to coach. Kids are going to have differences. When they're young, some days you might as well put on the striped shirt and hang a whistle around your neck. You'll be breaking up fights and making judgment calls all day.

As they get older, you'll do a lot less of that—but you'll do more coaching. When there is friction between them, it doesn't always help to jump in and restore peace. "Let the boys work that out between them," Cheryl would often tell me. And usually they did. Help your kids learn to work things out. Train them to see things from a perspective other than just their own. Encourage them to respond in love.

Help them understand that they're all different—for a reason. I took three pieces of wood and started cutting into them with a power jigsaw while my boys watched. Chunks of wood dropped to the floor until I was left with one piece of wood from each board.

I explained that the remaining pieces of wood were like them. Each of them started as a plain board. But after cutting into them like I did, all of them looked totally different. One became a cane. Another a candleholder. And the third was a simple wedge to prop open a door.

I explained that even though we're in the same family, God has different plans for each of us. So he'll often cut some things out of our life that don't belong there until we're perfectly suited to do the job he has for us.

> *The cane.* Maybe one of them will be the kind of person who supports others. Encourages them. Keeps others from falling.
>
> *The candleholder.* Maybe one of them will have a way of showing people the way…the light. Encouraging people in the Word. Sharing wisdom.
>
> *The door wedge.* Maybe one of them will be the kind of person who can open doors for others. Make things happen or provide opportunities others would never have had otherwise.

The point is, sometimes we need to remind our kids that they're all going to be different—partly due to the plan God has for them. Instead of letting these differences form divisions between the kids, help them embrace (or at least accept) the differences.

One of the best ways to do this is to take time occasionally to talk to each of your kids individually. Go out for some fast food. Let them vent. Then help them learn to love their siblings.

Help each of your kids see how they're different. How they're special. How God may be preparing them for something special later. Sometimes the tension between kids stems from jealousy. If we can help each of our kids recognize some of their own unique strong points, some of that jealousy may fade.

Avoid careless words. One of the toughest areas has to be the careless things that are said in a family, especially between siblings. Sarcasm. Insults. Hurtful criticism. Intimidation. You can do a lot to set the tone in this department—starting with how you talk to your wife and kids.

I did a number of family devotions with our kids to help encourage them to talk nicely to each other. Now I do similar object lessons with our high school seniors small group. One of my favorites is done with a gallon-size plastic bag filled with large chunks of gravel, marbles, or some of those smooth river stones you'd put in a fish tank. I pass the bag of rocks around and let the kids poke holes into it with a nail.

I hold up the bag.

"How many rocks did we lose?"

The answer is obvious. None.

"Wow, this bag is great. I didn't lose one rock. Not one."

They agree. Now I have one of the kids hold the mouth of the plastic bag open while I pour a pitcher of water into it. The bag spurts water in all directions.

"Ah, so the bag isn't in as good a shape as we thought."

Then I go on to explain how family members often take shots at each other. To hurt. Pay back. Get a laugh. Or sometimes we simply make careless, thoughtless comments. Family members know one another's weak points—which makes them easy targets. Often the person we jabbed acts like it didn't hurt them at all. They put up a front. But in reality, often we do great harm to each other. Is that what we want? Really?

> The words of the reckless pierce like swords, but the tongue
> of the wise brings healing (Proverbs 12:18).

What a great verse. One I try to live by. Do I want to be the person who gets the laugh by humiliating someone else? Do I want to be the guy who gets the dig in there—just to make me feel superior in some way? No thanks. I'm done with that stuff. I've set my heart on being someone who brings healing by the things I say.

Cultivate a spirit in your kids that seeks to strengthen and encourage their brothers and sisters. I think this is part of the reason I can't stand most sitcoms—especially those depicting family situations. They're full of dumb, selfish dads. Husbands and wives continually spar with each other. Kids dish out snappy one-liners and insults to their parents and each other. It's all about one-upping each other. We don't want that type of atmosphere in our homes.

As the kids grow up, there'll be a whole new dynamic when it comes to relating with adult siblings. With our three sons grown, sometimes I'll hear that a couple of them are having a "brothers day." A time to hang out, grab a meal, watch a movie, reconnect. That's good stuff. Encourage that in your family.

Before your kids grow up, you'll do well to take a look at how you relate to your siblings. Reestablish contact. Be there for them. Love them despite their quirks. Work toward family peace. Seek to show love to each other. Encourage each other. Your kids need to see that example. In other words, if you want your kids to get along with each other as adults, be sure you're making the effort with your own siblings and your wife's family. That isn't easy. Oftentimes that means you're going to be the one holding the shovel at the circus—behind the elephants. You know what I'm talking about. To the best of your ability, take the high road—not the route of the high and mighty. It's a great demonstration to our kids as well.

> Do not repay anyone evil for evil. Be careful to do what
> is right in the eyes of everyone. If it is possible, as far as
> it depends on you, live at peace with everyone (Romans
> 12:17-18).

Our adult kids will have times when they're irritated with each other. Or they'll have differences of opinion that may drive a wedge between them. My wife and I are firm believers that we'd better set the example by working hard to get along with others in our extended family—even if they're not meeting us halfway.

When an extended family "problem" came up, we'd often explain the situation to our kids and show them how we were choosing to work through it in love. This makes for good teaching time with the kids. As they grow, they'll know they're going to have to *work* to keep family relations good. I believe God will honor that work. Differences are bound to come between them, but hopefully not for long. Family needs to be there for each other.

Remember, home needs to be a haven. A safe place. A place where each family member can find peace, strength, and encouragement. Home should be free from things like selfishness, anger, jealousy, and meanness. They're sin. They're animals—and animals belong in a cage, not in your home.

Home Is a Hangout

Making sure your home is a safe haven is important—but you can't raise kids in a completely protected bubble. As kids get older, their friends will likely influence their decisions more than you will. Scary thought.

As parents, we need to be involved in our kids' world—and especially in their world of friends. When your kids develop close friendships at church you'll have plenty of opportunities to know their friends and their parents. You'll have a much better chance of encouraging the good friendships and minimizing the potential ill effects of others.

To be involved in your kids' world of friends, make your home a hangout. We wanted our kids to invite friends over. Encouraged it. Cheryl kept the freezer and fridge stocked with food and snacks. We learned the kids' names. Spent time talking to them and getting to know them. This doesn't sound like a big deal, but if you put it on a scale, it would weigh in at a much more impressive number than you think.

Sometimes Cheryl baked when kids were over. She's had other parents ask about her chocolate chip recipe or cupcake recipe—because their kids raved about them so much. Besides using fresh ingredients, her great secret to baking is simple. She makes them with love. Okay, that sounds sappy, I know. And she'll tear up when she reads this, but it's absolutely true. She bakes and does things to show kids she loves them, and the kids know it.

Get involved where your kids are. When our middle son was on the basketball team, Cheryl baked cookies for the entire team on game days. A little extra energy went a long way. At one sports honors banquet the team called her up and gave her an award. She got involved in PTA when the kids were in elementary school. She knew the kids to encourage friendships with and those to avoid. She knew many of the parents, too.

And put in some personal effort. Cheryl drove tons of kids to our church club program for years. In fact, there were times she had to swing by church on her way home from work to pick up a church van so she could bring all the kids into the Awana program at night.

I know some women thought she was crazy. Driving into Chicago during rush hour with a van full of kids? But she drove that van and listened. The kids often forgot she was there. They talked and talked, and Cheryl learned a lot about them and how to relate better. Crazy? Try *brilliant*.

As our kids' friends became more comfortable with us they were more likely to stop over. We could influence *these* kids for good—which helped our own kids as well.

Our kids didn't ask to spend a lot of time at friends' homes. And that was okay with us. How could we really monitor what was going on there? Our kids preferred being at our house—and so did their friends. That's exactly what you want.

There are downsides to having the home that kids like to come to. It's louder. It needs more cleanup and repairs. And the grocery bill was higher. But the payoff? Huge. Your home is a haven of protection. That's exactly what it should be. And sometimes the best way to protect your kids is to make your home a hangout so you know their friends—and so you can influence their friend decisions. Whoever thought stocking the fridge could be so important to good parenting?

Dating and Your Kids

Talking to kids about dating isn't a picnic, but I managed to work it around food. I took my oldest out to Chili's. After ordering, I pulled out a rattrap. You know, the type with the wooden base and the metal kill bar with coiled springs around it. Just like the old-fashioned mousetraps—only a lot more powerful.

I'd written lies about sex all over the trap with a fine point marker. I carefully set the trap and let it sit there on the table, hoping the waitress wouldn't stop by and see it. Then we talked about the lies. Things the world promotes about sex before marriage. Things our kids hear from friends.

For every lie I wrote the truth just below it—things that happen if you ignore God's plan and open the wedding gift early.

It's safe!

Actually, it can be deadly.

You can handle it!

But it may cripple you in many ways.

It feels great!

True, but outside of God's plan, it'll cause great pain.

It'll satisfy you—guaranteed!

Actually, you'll probably have many regrets.

You'll be glad you did it!

But you'll feel terrible guilt.

It'll give you thrills—and be exciting!

But at a high price.

This is living!
   Yeah, but something will die, too.
Enjoy your freedom!
   But this will enslave you like only sin can.
Nobody will ever know.
   You *will* be found out.
   "The devil always wants you looking at the bait—in this case, sex before marriage," I said. "And he surrounds the bait with lots of believable lies. He's hoping you don't know the truth, don't believe it, or ignore it."
   Then I jabbed the bait pad with a pencil, triggering the trap. The pencil shattered.
   "Sex is God's wedding gift. It's meant for marriage. But if you buy into the devil's lies and get involved in sex before marriage, it turns into a trap that can really hurt you."
   The dating years are a minefield, and we need to help our kids get through this phase safely. You've walked that field before. Learned hard lessons. You need to help your kids navigate it now. And let's face it: We've all seen kids that are forever changed—for the worse—because of dating choices. You've got a tough job ahead of you. No pressure.

What's dating all about?

   There are whole books about dating. Some want to embrace dating, others kiss it goodbye. But don't make this more complicated than it is. Dating is about finding the person you'll commit your entire life to—and about preparing for that lifetime together. Make sure your kids understand that. Dating isn't a cultural thing we do just to have fun. There's a purpose behind it.

How old should your kids be before they date?

   Tough question. The answer varies depending on how mature your kids are. How trustworthy. How committed to purity and God's standards they really are. One of my daughters-in-law couldn't date until she turned eighteen. It was a family rule. It wasn't a problem with her. In fact, it worked really well.

And I could also make a case for dating slightly younger than that. I started dating my wife when I was seventeen—in the fall of my senior year in high school. Cheryl was sixteen—a junior. One thing I like about allowing dating at seventeen is that as parents we're around to monitor things. We're there to talk after a date and help process what happened. We're there to ask the tough questions and make sure they're not crossing boundaries. We'll know who they're dating and will spend time with them. If they don't start dating until they go to college, you'll lose opportunities to guide and influence them while they date.

When I see the maturity level of many sixteen-year-olds, I honestly would question the sanity of letting them date that young. And dating younger than that—in our culture today—is nuts. Okay, let me be more tactful. I think it would be risky. As a parent, sometimes you need to make unpopular decisions in order to protect your kids. Remember, dating isn't just a fun social activity. It is about finding a mate—and fifteen sounds a bit young.

If your kids are younger, set up a family standard that lets the kids know years in advance when dating can begin. Hey, write it out and post it. Do this long before they reach the dating years and you'll save yourself a lot of conflict later. Here's a sample.

In our house, dating can't begin until you're at least seventeen—and even then, only if you've demonstrated you're ready to date. Here are things I'll be looking for.

Mature attitude. Understanding dating is about finding a person you'll commit your entire life to.

Solid commitment. To conduct yourself in a manner that is pleasing to God in all areas—including purity and dressing modestly and appropriately.

Sound judgment. The person you pick to go out with must pass our standards. If you're not choosing wisely in this area, you're not ready to date.

Trustworthy track record. We'll be trusting you with curfews, conduct, honesty, and more. We'll need to see a history of trustworthiness.

Open communication. We'll need to see that you'll be open with us and willing to talk about your relationships. If you're secretive, you're not ready to date. And when you come home from dates, you'll be expected to talk with us about it. We're not trying to pry—we're trying to protect.

Meet the date. *We need to meet the date beforehand.*

Usually we'd know who the girl was already—because they were from church. My wife and I only had boys, but if I had a daughter, I'd definitely throw one more thing in there.

The boy needs to get my permission to ask you out. *I need to meet the boy who wants to take you out. He'll need to ask me to take you out, face-to-face, and we're going to spend a little time talking together before I'll agree to it.*

More about this later.

Who do you date?

A committed Christian, for starters. And understand, if you and your mate are Christians but your marriage is mediocre, the whole bit about dating a Christian will be a much tougher sell.

Talk about the type of person your kids are to date long before they're old enough to date. We've helped our kids see the critical importance of dating only Christians. Every year I talk to our high school small group about this. And to illustrate it, I ask them to pair up for a three-legged race through an obstacle course—for time. Then each couple runs the course again, but this time one of the team members stands backward when they lace up together. You can imagine how much longer it takes them to do it this way.

I ask them to imagine there is a three-legged cross-country race with a $1,000,000 prize for every couple who crosses the finish line within a set amount of time. If they entered that race, how would they lace up? Both facing the same direction—or one turned 180 degrees the wrong way? Naturally, they'd want to face the same direction for the best shot at the prize.

Marriage can be like a three-legged marathon over rough terrain. Any Christian couple can have a $1,000,000 marriage—if both are going in the same direction. But if one is a Christian and the other isn't, there'll be problems.

> The sinful nature wants to do evil, which is just the oppo-
> site of what the Spirit wants. And the Spirit gives us desires
> that are the opposite of what the sinful nature desires. These
> two forces are constantly fighting each other, so you are not
> free to carry out your good intentions (Galatians 5:17 NLT).

The thing that trips up many Christians dating a non-Christian is that they feel so close. And they are. Whether I lace up in that three-legged race facing the same direction or not, I am just as close either way. But it can't stay that way. This is the truth that kids miss.

Even though a Christian and a non-Christian can feel close, they are going in opposite directions. One has the Spirit. The other only has the old nature. And the Spirit will be giving the Christian new desires. No matter how wonderful the non-Christian mate is, it will be very hard for them to stay close. In the long run, a relationship between a Christian and a non-Christian is doomed to be less than a marriage should be. Either the Christian will drift from their mate or drift from the Lord. Either is disastrous. This is why the Bible warns us in 2 Corinthians 6:14, "Do not be yoked together with unbelievers."

It can be easy to get close to someone—and to fall in love. Protect your kids by establishing a family standard that they only date Christians. Remember, dating is about finding a person to marry, not just something kids do for fun.*

Date a person with the right heart. Every year we take our high school seniors small group to a used car lot and give them ten minutes to pick out their dream car or truck. Price was no object, because we weren't buying anything.

After the kids made their decisions, each had the chance to show the rest of the group his choice and explain why they picked it. Often guys say things like, "I just really like the way this car looks." "It's really fast." "I can imagine what my friends will say when I pull up in this." Girls usually say, "I just think it looks cute" or "I really like this color."

---

* This is the short version of "The Three-legged Race Case," a devotional found in *Dangerous Devotions for Guys*. It was written for youth leaders, but adapts easily for family use. Check out the complete devotional, and you'll get another twenty-three in the book you can use as well.

Now we go get something to eat and talk about it. I point out that nobody said, "This is the car I like, but we'd probably want a mechanic to look at it if we were really going to buy it. A look under the hood is important if you want the car to go the distance, right?" They'd all agree to that. Now it's time to transition to spiritual truth.

Sometimes we choose someone we'd like to date in the same way we picked the car we'd like to drive. "He's so cute." "I like how she looks." Often we base our decisions on surface stuff. But if we want that relationship to go the distance, we need to know about the engine that *drives* them. We need to know about their heart. And who is the only one that knows a person's heart? Ah yes, that would be God.*

Prepping your daughter for dating

There's a problem with "Daddy/Daughter" dates. The whole idea behind this is to help a girl know how a man should treat a girl on a date. Now, I think Dad ought to have one-on-one time with each of his kids—daughters *and* sons. A time to go out and talk. See where they're at. Encourage them. Listen. Keep your bond tight.

But I wouldn't call it a "date." It's totally unrealistic. Your daughter is going out with her *dad*. I'm not sure how much that will prepare them for going out with a teenage guy with racing hormones.

If you want to show your daughter how a girl should be treated, let her tag along occasionally when you're taking your wife on a date. Let her see how the two of you talk and listen to each other. How you show each other affection. How you respect and treasure each other. And if you're not dating your wife—why would you take your daughter on a date? To show her how special you *used* to treat your wife? Your wife is your number one. Reserve the dating budget for her.

Whether you date your daughter or not, be sure you're telling your daughter that you love her and *how* she's beautiful. Compliment her on her character. Her heart. Her good qualities—not just her outward beauty. These are areas any girl can develop to become more and more

---

* We encourage kids to ask God to lead them to the person with the right heart. This is a powerful thing to do with your kids. You'll find the complete devotional, "Beauty is a Beast," in *Dangerous Devotions for Guys*.

attractive. Give her frequent hugs. Show her *and* tell her you love her. You don't want your daughter so starved for affection that she'll fall for the first guy who gives her a little attention.

Prepping your son for dating

Give your boy some conversational coaching. Give him tips for talking to a girl. And for listening. A date gets extra awkward when couples run out of things to talk about. Help him brainstorm questions he can ask the girl. Encourage him to ask about her interests, dreams, her life, family, past. Some guys go on a date and only want to talk about themselves.

Remind him of common courtesies and basic responsibilities. Opening her door. You know this stuff. Being mindful of danger— because on a date, he's the protector. He needs to think about where he's taking her. Is it a safe place? Does he have plenty of gas in the car? Does he know how to get where he's going?

And talk to him about being a man of honor. About boundaries he shouldn't cross physically. See all the fun things you get to do as a parent? My wife and I have said it many times…the dating years are highly overrated.

Your daughter and dressing for the date

She wants to look pretty. Attractive. Yes, of course. But she needs to understand the whole modesty thing, too. Hopefully you're reading this well in advance of her dating years so you can address modesty when she's young. Then, when it comes to the dating years she'll be ready. She'll understand.

If your daughter is pushing to date now and you've not talked with her about modesty—you'll need to have a good talk with her. Oh boy.

Here's what I'd suggest. Pick up a dozen donuts from Krispy Kreme—or someplace where the boxes have a big cellophane window to view the delicious donuts inside. Then pick up a dozen donuts from Dunkin' Donuts—or someplace local that offers the donuts in a box *without* a window.

Use the boxes to illustrate how guys are visual. When guys look at the box from Krispy Kreme they're focused on the donuts they see through that window. And when a girl wears a tight-fitting or low-cut top, guess what the guy is looking at. The donuts.

Your daughter wants her date to be focused on her, on who she is—not on her body. *Don't give a guy a window.* Don't wear something that is going to arouse him more than he already is. The same goes for clothes that fit tight around the hips.

This is especially important when it comes to formal dances. The dresses girls wear are unbelievable. They are *unbelievable.* When I see couples dressed for an event like this, there are questions rolling in my mind. Here's the big one. *How did a dad let his girl out of the house wearing that dress?*

If she's wearing an open, low-cut back that shows a lot of skin, she's instantly clued her date into one arousing fact. *No bra.* Then the front. Often the dress is strapless with cups the girls are constantly pulling up and adjusting—as if the cleavage alone wasn't enough to keep their date's eyes glued there. If you're going to let your girl go to prom, be real about the dress. A revealing one is a tease to a guy—and for some, a challenge. Do you really want your girl wearing a dress that is going to sexually arouse her date?

There's a big difference between dressing in an *attractive* way and an *arousing* way. Finding a modest dress—or altering it so it is—can be done, but it may not be popular with your daughter. But if you've already established a commitment to modesty with her, it'll help.

Where to go and what to do on a date

Okay, this is tough, because I can't possibly cover everything. The real point of this section is to be sure you've covered the topic with your daughters *and* sons.

Just the two of them. In a crowded restaurant? No problemo. Sitting in a car, their date's house, apartment, dorm—or even your house when nobody else is home? No way.

Dancing. I don't want to sound all legalistic here. Just *realistic.* When a girl is dancing with a guy, his physical arousal goes through the roof. If she's dancing close, just the feel of her body moving and rubbing against his body will definitely stoke the flames of desire. You want that to happen?

What if the dancing won't involve being close? Which means a girl is standing eighteen inches in front of a guy. Her body swaying with the rhythm of the music. *That's* arousing. If the music is faster, the girl's body will be shaking in all the right places. Where will your son be looking—or the guy dancing with your daughter? At the donuts.

I recently heard someone say, "Dancing is a prelude to sex." Oh, yeah. I can see that. My opinion? Save the dancing for the wedding. And after the kids are married, hey, they can take classes if they want. Become a regular Bojangles. Dance the night away. Dance between the sheets.

Movies. Two concerns. First, if the movie shows skin, or sexual situations, this may increase a guy's appetite and lower a girl's inhibitions. Not a great combination for a date. They need to choose responsibly. The other concern is that if they're doing *too* much movie watching, they aren't talking and getting to know each other.

Encourage your son or daughter to spend time with their date's family. When you marry somebody, it's a package deal. You get their family too. They need to see if that can work.

Encourage them to spend time at your house. You'll want to get to know the date, and for them to know you. You'll want to see how the two of them relate as they play games, talk, or just hang out.

What do they need to be learning about their date?

Dating should be fun—of course. But they aren't going out just to have fun. Dating is about two people seeing if they're right for each other.

Their level of commitment to Christ. How real is it? Not just in the way they talk, but how they live it out. The stronger the commitment, the more likely they'll follow God's principles for marriage—even when they may not feel like it. When looking for a mate, that's good information to know.

Their character. How committed are they to integrity? Honesty? Are they a complainer? A whiner? Argumentative? Controlling? Selfish?

Their "hero status." Do they do the right thing, even when it's hard? Are they making genuine efforts to follow God's plan for life?

How do they treat others? Strangers. Friends. Parents. Siblings. Their date.

What are their opinions on important issues? What would they go to the mat for, and what would they feel isn't worth fighting for or over?

You get the idea. There's plenty to learn about each other.

Know the plan

As a dad, it's important to know where they're going for the date. *What restaurant? How long will they be there? Then what?*

This is about their protection. If you make hearing the date plan part of your standard operating procedure, it shouldn't be a big deal.

Limitations

We limited the number of dates our kids went on and how much time they spent on the phone with girlfriends during a week. Your teen still needs to function as a brother, sister, son, daughter, worker, student, and church member. Help them learn balance.

How far to go on a date

Make sure your kids know the boundaries and are truly committed to staying within them before they date. Sex is great—when we follow God's plan. And sex bonds two people together. Unfortunately some bond with people they never marry, and then wonder why the bond isn't as close with the person they *do* marry.

Kissing. Make sure you've talked to your kids about French kissing in plain English. It's wonderfully arousing—which is great in marriage. It's part of foreplay. But when you're dating, it's playing with fire.

Touching. I've told high school kids to imagine someone of the opposite sex fully dressed. They're wearing full-length jeans and a short-sleeved shirt. Basic principle? Don't touch what is covered with clothes. Never, ever unbutton, unzip, take off, pull down, pull up, or slip your hand underneath your date's clothing—and don't let your date do it to you.

Tell guys... Legs, thighs, butt, breasts, and everything in between are off-limits. They aren't yours to touch—even if a girl wants you to. You answer to God, not her.

Tell girls... Be careful about touching a guy *anywhere*. Laying your hand on his thigh while you're watching a movie can arouse him more than you know. And be careful of any suggestive comments or overly flirtatious behavior. Guys can get the wrong signal. He's seeing a green light, and he's ready to step on the gas.

And one more thought here. Early on, explain that living together before marriage is wrong. Our culture tries to make it look okay. Responsible. Like it's about being sure you're compatible. *Bunk.*

Living together is about having sex without fully committing to the other person. Sounds more like it's a form of using someone. Doesn't that make you feel special? Sex before marriage is just plain old sin—and always a bad idea.

Some brilliant dating logic

John Van Epp, PhD, wrote a book entitled *How to Avoid Marrying a Jerk*. He outlines a rational approach to the whole physical end of things in dating. The logic goes something like this.

Would you trust a person you didn't know? Of course not.

Would you rely on a person you didn't trust? Ridiculous.

Would you commit to a person you couldn't rely on? That's insane.

Would you let someone touch you sexually before you knew you could trust them or rely on them or before they've committed to you? Not a chance. That's a formula for heartache and regret.

The point is that dating is a progression that is supposed to lead to a marriage commitment, and *then* sex. Get the order wrong and you'll have a mess. Before you start dating someone, you get to know as much about that person as you possibly can. If they pass that test, only then do you go to the dating stage. When you're dating, you're determining if this date is someone you can trust. This has to do with their character, integrity, commitment to Christ, and more. And if they're trustworthy, you begin to rely on them, which will reveal more and more if they are truly trustworthy or not. As things progress, you begin to commit to that person in increasingly greater ways. Eventually, that leads to marriage—and *then* sex.

Meeting with your daughter's potential date

I don't have daughters, but if I did, this would be an absolute. A must. A nonnegotiable. You're entrusted with protecting your daughter. And before you let some guy you don't know take her out for an evening, have a little face time with him.

Ideally, long before she's old enough to date, your daughter should understand that this will be part of the process. That'll save you from arguments about it when she's ga-ga about some guy. She needs to know that you're the gatekeeper—and there are some things that simply need to be understood. The guy needs to ask you for permission to take your daughter out. The guy needs to talk to you in person—face to face. You'll need to go over some things with him…and only if he passes your interview will she go out with him.

If your daughter is of dating age now and you decide to institute this requirement, don't expect her to do cartwheels. She may fear it will scare guys away. But you've got an answer for that. If a guy isn't willing to do that for your daughter, he isn't worthy of her.

Bruce Olson met with my oldest son, Andy, before Andy could date their daughter, Laura. The Olsons had established dating rules, and this was one of them. Bruce gave Andy a little questionnaire to fill out and bring to the meeting. Bruce also had a little required reading for Andy to do ahead of time. Brilliant moves on his part. Bruce cared enough about Laura to be sure she was protected. He wanted to make sure Andy would love God and respect Laura enough to do things right.

Andy passed the interview stage. But Bruce stayed involved. Occasionally he met Andy for breakfast, just the two of them, to talk man-to-man. Bruce did it right.

If I had a daughter, I'd do the same thing. I'd meet with him. I wouldn't intimidate the guy. Not at all. I'd want to start building a relationship with him. I'd want to get to know him as a man and begin to earn his respect. Remember, if he respects me, he'll be less likely to rebel against our family standards, too. He'd know how much I love my daughter, and that when he's out with her, he's taking my place as her protector in every way. I think it is important to treat him like a man—and a guy with the right character will rise to the occasion. I'd give him my phone number and ask him to call me if he needed any-thing—or if he was running late getting my daughter home. He'll get the message I'm going to stay involved with my daughter, and with him—in a good way.

But I'd do this in a nice way. Not belittling. Not controlling. Hey, this guy might be my son-in-law someday. I'd treat him with respect. Treat him like a man.

If they continued dating I'd do just what Bruce Olson did with my son. We'd go out for breakfast occasionally and talk. I'd want to be a part of his life. I'd want to listen to him and help lead him on the high road. And I hope you'll do that, too.

Protecting your daughter from an aggressive guy

Dr. Jekyll and Mr. Hyde. There are guys who seem like a gentleman, but on a date they morph into something horrible. A monster with eight hands. Some guys will tell a girl *anything* just to try to get physi-cal with her. You've warned your daughter about that, right?

What if your daughter's date gets handsy or aggressive on the date? Work through scenarios with your daughter. Play "what if" games.

"What if your date acts like he loves you, but wants you to prove your love for him?"

"What if your date buys you a nice dinner and feels you owe him dessert?"

"What if your date seems aggressive, and deep inside you feel a little fear, a warning?"

"What if your date tries to convince you that it's okay to break the rules just a little?"

Have your daughter talk through her course of action in each of these scenarios and others you may come up with. Make sure she understands how real and prevalent date rape is—or something close to it. Many, many girls are pressured into sex on some level—don't let your daughter be one of them. Be sure she always has a phone on her. If she has an uneasy feeling, encourage her to follow her instinct. But asking the date to take her home may be risky. Better that she asks to stop in a restroom and sneaks her phone out to call you from there. Then she stays put until you get there. Let her know that you'll pick her up—anytime, night or day.

Protecting your son from an aggressive girl

A guy needs to be just as careful. If his date wants to get physical, encourage your son to be a Joseph and run. Some girls want to feel loved. Others want a trophy—and your son is it. Some girls want to build a reputation, destroying your son's in the process.

A girl might tempt your son to cross some boundaries. Encourage him to end the date pronto, talk to you about it, and not date the girl again. What he's got is worth protecting and saving for the girl who will commit to him for a lifetime.

The dating years. Not the easiest phase of your parenting journey. But don't slack off. This is when kids can get really hurt and damaged. Be sure you're "on your toes" and on your knees.

The Fight for Independence

Cheryl and I keep the house pretty chilly in the winter—especially at night. Now, imagine us climbing in bed and me pulling the comforter off Cheryl in my attempt to get warm. But she's cold, too, so she pulls the comforter off me and onto herself. We're wasting energy fighting for covers when in reality we both want the exact same thing.

We want to stay warm.

Fighting for what we want is pointless. If we move closer together, we'll both have what we need.

Maybe that's a goofy example, but there's a lesson in it when it comes to handling the tension that develops between teens and their parents in the fight for independence.

Our children want independence and to be treated like adults—not kids. Independence is a natural desire that wells up in our kids. And it's a good thing. You don't want your kids living with you when they're thirty. You want them to leave the nest. To fly. To find a good mate. Raise a family. To be a good Christian man or woman. That's what you were aiming for, right?

The fact is this. Your teens want the same thing. They want to be free, and you want to let them go. You're on the same side. Your job is to communicate that to them clearly. You'll need to reinforce the message many times and in a number of ways. The more successful you are in conveying this message to them, the less conflict you'll have between you. The message is simple. They won't have to fight you for independence; you'll be giving it to them.

Trust is the key thing for them to understand. Trust is the doorway to freedom.

Dad gives a little responsibility. They follow through. Trust increases.

They're faced with right and wrong. They choose right. Trust increases.

They have to make a decision. They choose wisely. Trust increases.

They face some kind of test. They prove reliable. Trust increases.

And as trust increases, we give them more leash. More freedom. That's how it works. That's what we need our kids to understand.

You and your teens want the same thing. They want to be free, and you want to let them go. You're on the same side.

It's like the parables Jesus told of the man who entrusted his property and money to his servants. Those who were trustworthy, reliable, and faithful were rewarded. It works the same way with our kids.

And the converse is true. The more our kids are untrustworthy, the more they prove they don't have the maturity or haven't developed the character and responsibility to be trusted more. So we have to pull in the leash.

The more the kids understand this, the better. They don't want to be treated like kids. And we don't want to treat them like that either. We want to encourage our kids to mature, to show they are responsible, and to grow in the Lord. And as they do, better things—like freedoms—would come as a result.

The point is this. Don't get into a fight for independence in your home. Like that example of Cheryl and me and the comforter. When two people want the same thing, the best thing they can do is stay close and work for it together.

One Thing

For family devotions next week, how about we go to the stock car races?" My boys thought that sounded like a great idea. And a week later we sat on the bleachers of a local Wisconsin oval track taking it all in.

We did what most guys do at an event like this. On the opening lap each of us picked a car we hoped would win. And after they waved the green flag we hoped for a little bumping and sliding action, especially on the turns.

On the drive home I asked the guys to tell me what they saw. To boil it all down. They said something like this. "A bunch of guys driving around in a circle, trying to get ahead of each other."

Bingo. I had the opportunity to drive home the point.

"That's exactly how most men live their entire life. They're going around in circles. Trying to get ahead. Trying to get the advantage over others. But in the end, they end up right where they started."

The boys were quiet.

"God has a different plan for you, guys. He won't send you in circles. He's got a journey for each of you, if you'll take it. You'll bump others. Not to get ahead of them—but to impact them for Christ. It's my prayer that you take that road, and don't settle for the racetrack."

As dads, this is part of our job. To lead them on a different route than the world chooses. To help our kids become men and women of integrity. Adults who love God and love others. Mates who will love their spouse and their kids.

Let's talk about some things that I think our kids truly need if we want to keep them on the right track.

One thing our sons and daughters must know.

One thing they must hear from you.

One thing they must understand.

One thing they must accept.

One Thing They Must Know

"When will I be a man? When will I be a woman?"

The world stands ready to answer this question for them. The world has a short list of things that determine when you're a man or a woman.

When your body matures.

When you take your first drink.

When you reach eighteen, or twenty-one.

When you get a job—or your own apartment.

When you can drive a car—or better yet, own one.

When you have sex.

These are the messages your kids get. Unless you tell them what an adult really is, they'll likely attempt to affirm they're a man or a woman in one of the above ways. Deep down they need to prove it to themselves and to the world around them.

This is a problem in our society. I believe this is why some men in their midlife look for a new career, a new car, or a new woman. These were the types of things they thought were part of proving themselves to be a man when they were teenagers. Now, when their middle has gone soft and they aren't feeling much like a man, they go back to old ways to try to prove it. I imagine a similar thing happens to women.

When will I be a man? Here's one way I helped answer that question for my boys. I had a "Rite of Passage" night for each of them when they were eighteen. I invited probably twenty-five men. Grandpas, uncles, friends of mine, pastors—men I respected in their walk with Christ. When my second son had his night, Andy, his older brother, was there. And when it was Luke's turn, both older brothers were part of the group.

I asked each man to write a letter to my son telling him about something they learned as a man, or something they felt was important that he know. And I asked them to bring some little token to go along with it. Nothing expensive—just a visual reminder of the lesson they wanted to get across to my son.

The night of the event, we had pizza and each man read his letter to our son. The letter was put in a sheet protector and then into a three-ring binder for our son. Man after man came up, sharing some bit of wisdom as they welcomed my son into the brotherhood of men.

We confirmed that night that he was a man. He didn't have to try to prove it with some feat or exploit. He was a man. A young man, but a man. On a man's journey. The real question wasn't, "When will I be a man?" anymore, but rather "What kind of man will I choose to be?" After the letters, we sat him in a chair and the men gathered around to pray over him. One young man surrounded by men of all ages. Each of us encouraged my sons, in our own way, to be a hero. A man who did the right things and didn't give up—even when that was hard. A man who chose to do life God's way, with his help.

> The real question wasn't, "When will I be a man?" anymore, but rather "What kind of man will I choose to be?"

A Rite of Passage night is a powerful event. And if I had daughters, I'd have done the same thing for them. I want to encourage you to do this for your kids.

One Thing They Must Hear from You

"I'm proud of you."

Deep down it's one of their deepest cravings. They want your approval. Need it. *Give it to them.* Let them know that you love and respect them, but don't stop there. They must know you're proud of them.

This is what God did right after Jesus's baptism in the Jordan River.

> And a voice from heaven said, 'This is my Son, whom I love; with him I am well pleased" (Matthew 3:17).

God got it all in there. The fact that he loved Jesus. The fact that he was pleased with him. Which all boiled down to the fact that God was proud to call Jesus His son.

We can do the same for our kids. I used this very scripture in the closing prayer to each of my boys at their Rite of Passage night.

And we need to affirm this in everyday life. Not just when they make a great sports play. Not just for a good grade on an exam. But for those times when...

- they make a wise decision.

- they choose right over wrong.

- they prove responsible.

- they treat their mom with respect.

- they show love.

- they do the right thing, even when it is hard.

- they work hard.

- they show great self-control.

- they don't give up, even though a lesser person would have.

"I'm proud of you." They need to hear it. Let them hear it from *you*.

One Thing They Must Understand

"You'll soon be free to make your own choices."

We covered this pretty well in the last chapter, so we don't need to rehash it here. But it belongs on this short list of things our kids need to know or hear—especially from their dad. You don't want your kids fighting you to try to win independence. You want them to use their "fight" for good things, like learning self-control, making wise choices, and gaining trust and freedom in the process.

Freedom is sacred. Help your kids see this. The freedom to choose is a privilege of adulthood. The decision to follow God's ways is the mark of one choosing wisely.

Yes, your kids need to know freedom is coming—and that you're preparing them to be free. Often they'll want to stretch their wings. Flex their muscles. They'll be restless to do *something*. Encourage them to choose well.

One Thing They Must Accept

"Being a man or a woman doesn't mean you must do it alone."

This was another lesson we taught during the Rite of Passage night. I'd stacked a couple storage bins on one side of the room. After all the letters were read, and just before we celebrated with dessert, we gathered all the men together to watch.

I asked my son to carry each of the bins to the other side of the room.

The men watched in silent curiosity as my son picked up the first bin and carried it across the room. He set it down and went back for the second one.

When he tried to pick it up, the thing wouldn't budge. Before anyone had arrived, I'd filled it with sand. The thing weighed a ton.

He struggled for a moment and glanced up at me—a little confusion on his face.

"I asked you to carry it to the other side of the room, but I didn't say you couldn't ask for help."

He grinned. "Anybody want to give me a hand?"

Men stepped forward—eager to pitch in. Together they hoisted the bin high and walked it to the other side of the room.

"This was your final lesson of the night," I said. "Just because you're a man doesn't mean you can do everything on your own. You need to accept the fact that you can't. And that's okay. Reach out to other men for help and counsel and encouragement on your journey. And reach out to God for the same."

These are things our kids need to know.

That they're a man—or a woman. That your desire is for them to be God's man or woman.

That you're proud of them. That you love them and respect them.

That you're preparing them to be free. They'll be making all their own choices soon.

And finally, that God doesn't expect them to do it all on their own. You'll be there for them. Others will, too. And God himself will help them. All they need to do is ask.

Demonstrate these truths to them, and you'll be a hero. And you'll help them be one, too.

God Gives You Three Things

I'm going to lose my voice—to you, anyway. There's so much more to say, but we're nearing the end of the book. And so I write these last chapters of concluding thoughts on marriage and parenting with growing passion. A sense of urgency. Stick with me a little longer, okay?

We did a little family devotional with our boys as they were growing up, and now we do the same every year with our high school seniors small group.

The kids form teams of two or three, and we give each team five dollars. We go to the local grocery store and give them ten minutes to purchase anything to eat or drink that they want.

What do they buy? Chips. Pop. Candy. Yeah, junk food. I've never seen a teenager buy fresh fruit or vegetables, milk, or bread. Nothing with any real nutritional value.

I gave them time, resources, and the absolute freedom to choose whatever they wanted—and from a nutritional standpoint, they chose poorly. The activity triggered a talk about how we spend our lives.

As men, God gives us the same three things.

Time. God gives you time on earth—life itself. And he gives you a very limited amount of time with your kids.

Resources. God gives you resources. Money. Abilities. Opportunities. And in some ways I think these resources can include the kids themselves.

Freedom. God gives you a free will. The freedom to choose how you're going to live. How to spend your time and resources.

How are you using these three? Sometimes, just like kids picking junk food, we make choices that have no *spiritually* nutritional value. They hold no significant value for us or our kids. No real benefits now—or for eternity.

My three sons are grown men now. With that in mind, let me mention a few things that I can see clearly from my vantage point in life. Things that might influence how you use your time, resources, and freedom.

Going, going, gone

"Enjoy your kids now. They'll grow up before you know it." I heard that plenty of times as a young parent. We've all heard it. I just never believed it could be so quick.

See, it didn't seem that way. Not at first. That was the real fooler. I thought those older people who made that statement were wrong somehow. At least in our case. Cheryl and I were totally enjoying the kids.

But looking back, when the kids were born and even when they were toddlers, life was like a roller coaster on its first long climb. *Click-click-click-click.* Life was busy, but it didn't seem to be moving *too* fast. In fact, the speed seemed perfect. The coaster of parenthood was steadily climbing—and we loved it. We were enjoying every minute. Taking in the view.

But at some point things changed. Sometime after diapers, but long before dating. The pace picked up. Accelerated. The roller coaster was moving now. Faster and faster. Thrills. Chills. Lots of fun and laughs. We were absolutely loving it.

And then it was over.

The ride slowed down, and it was as if I looked over at the kids— but my boys weren't kids anymore. They were men. And all I kept thinking was *I want to do this again.* What a ride.

"Enjoy your kids now. They'll grow up before you know it." The old cliché is understated, if anything. Keep this in mind when you use your time.

Be smart about time-stealers, or love-leeches. They suck away chances to give and enjoy love as a family. Here are a few of them.

The Stupid Box

AKA the television. Be careful how much time you spend on it, or how much you use it to occupy the kids so you can "get things done." And this especially goes for the TVs built into the back of seats in cars. Use traveling time to talk to the kids.

Video Games

Same as above.

i-i-i

iPhones. iPods. iPads. Products and brand names will change, but don't let that outdate this principle. I'm talking about the latest technology, whatever it is. The stuff that's supposed to keep us connected, but in reality it keeps us disconnected from everything and everyone immediately around us. There's a reason all these things start with *I*. Because these things are generally all about "me." Not that you can't have these things. But be careful. They can bring you into your own little world, and that means you're not connecting with your kids.

And while I'm at it, buying anything for your kids that requires earbuds isn't entirely smart. They'll disengage. Buds are not your *buds*.

Think about it. If your kids are off in their own world, that means they're an alien, right? And they might as well be. They're not relating with you or anyone else.

Social Networking

When the kids are small, there isn't much time for you to do social networking of any kind. Sometimes you need to stop trying to be a social friend of hundreds of acquaintances and focus on the mate and family God has given to you. Obviously you'll want to monitor how much you let the kids use social networking, too.

Special Interests

I never picked up golf. I think I would have liked it and had offers to go, but I avoided it. Why? It would have taken me away from Cheryl and the kids for big chunks of time. I've never been sorry that I gave up golf before I started. I'm not saying "avoid golf." But think about what you're involved in, or what you're thinking of picking up. Will it add to your relationship with your mate and kids, or leech time away?

When that roller coaster is moving, you're so busy holding on and enjoying the ride that it might be over before you think about how you could have enjoyed it more. There are plenty of other time-stealers and love-leeches. Look for them and deal with them.

Find ways to spend real time with the kids instead. We made everything a game, from racing upstairs at bedtime to making our way through a mall by only stepping on certain colored tiles.

I was walking down a long terminal corridor of an airport recently. A couple walked toward me with a young boy in tow, holding his daddy's hand. The boy was maybe four or five years old. He was doing the tile thing. Stretching his strides to step only on certain colors. I smiled and watched—and wanted to join him. The dad was busy looking at illuminated advertisements on the walls. The mom was in her own world. I don't know what was going through their heads, but I remember exactly what was going through mine. *Look what your son is doing. Don't miss this. Play the game with him. This stage won't last long.*

And so I want to encourage you. Open your eyes. Find ways to connect with your kids. Engage them. Here are some suggestions. Some of these you'll probably think are crazy—and that's okay. But find your own things. These are just some things we did with our boys.

Books. Read to them. Some of my best memories are of reading to my kids—even as they got older. Glancing up and looking at their faces as they were drawn away into the wonder of some adventure—now that's priceless.

Movies. I'm not talking about using a movie as a babysitter. This is about making a special event by occasionally watching a movie together as a family. I took an old game table, the kind with the folding legs, and cut the legs down. I'd set it up in front of the TV so the kids could sit on the floor and eat pizza with the movie.

Errands. Running an errand? Take one of the kids with you. Sure it will slow you down—but you'll probably give your wife a breather.

Make it an adventure. I'd make the fish "talk" to one of my sons every time we went by that section at the grocery store. Turn strollers and shopping carts into racecars. Fishtail and slide into the turns. Top it off with sound effects. You may not move through your to-do list quite as fast, but you'll have more fun—and accomplish more in the long run—if you take kids with you.

Chores. Mowing the lawn? Take the kids along. They rode in a backpack when they were small. And when they got bigger, they used a toy mower. Sometimes we need to fight that urge to "get things done" and take time to enjoy the kids.

Break the rules. Turn your mattress into a trampoline. Sneak a snack to the kids after they're in bed. I used to have dates with Cheryl after the kids were in bed when they were young. We'd order chop suey and watch a movie downstairs. I'd always "sneak" a bowl up to the kids. By their reaction, you'd think I brought them a treasure box. And to me, the moment was gold.

Sometimes rules, like bedtime, should be broken when you have a good reason. Occasionally letting kids read a good book in bed with a flashlight is a perfectly good reason, the way I see it.

Throw a "midnight." Sometimes when I was playing catch with the kids, I'd call "midnight" and throw the football or baseball extra high. If they made that catch, they got to stay up until midnight sometime. Now, rarely did we ever stay up that late. But they got to stay up later—and they loved it.

Make a mess. Finger paint at the kitchen table. Carve pumpkins. Make batches of homemade play dough. Rake the leaves in a pile and let them play in them before you bag them up. You're not just making a mess, you're making memories—and the best ones usually require a little cleanup.

Double duty. Don't just clear snow off your drive. Shovel it into a big pile and make a snow fort. Now everybody is happy.

Snack run. Take the kids for impromptu runs to Dairy Queen, or to Wendy's for a Frosty, or wherever. I have an old pickup. We'd drive that in the summer, and the kids would sit in the bed eating while we were parked.

Vacation. If you can afford it, do it. And if you vacation to some touristy place, don't grumble about the price you're paying for a hamburger. You're on vacation. If the only reason you don't vacation is because you think you'll get behind at work, or that work can't make it without you, you'll totally regret it. If you can't afford a vacation, get creative. Go camping. Go to museums. Just spend time with the kids.

Celebrate. Find a reason to celebrate something...anything. Just got some good news? Declare a family holiday to celebrate.

Boating. Get out in a boat—and let them drive. Rent one for a day, or find a friend who has one and can take you for a ride. Snorkel with them and let them see the wonder of God's underwater world.

Take them there. Watch fireworks for real—not on television. Take them for a hike. Let them experience things, especially nature.

Get grass stains. Let the kids play, get dirty, and be kids. Wrestle with them. Grass stains are badges of honor. They're testaments to the fact that your kids are active and having fun.

Buy fireworks. And blow them off together. Dangerous? Sure. But it's a great chance to teach them to be safe. Nobody is more safety-conscious as a parent than me. But that doesn't mean you insulate them from dangerous things. Better yet, teach them how to handle dangerous things in a safe and responsible way.

Make a potato gun. Boys love it. *Love* it. If this is too much for you, skip to the next one and forget I ever mentioned it. But if you're still reading, you can find plans online. We had a riot with it. Blasting a potato against a big rock and getting instant mashed potatoes—you can't imagine the excitement.

We shot it out into a lake most of the time. On one occasion one of my nephews rowed out in a small boat, armed with a metal garbage lid for a shield. He stood up and taunted us. We fired. He moved the shield to deflect the flying potato—and it knocked him right into the water. Think the kids will forget that? Not hardly.

Forts and tunnels. Outdoors and indoors. Please, please don't miss the chance to make forts in the house. Couch cushions, blankets, chairs. We made elaborate tunnels in our basement and den and had a great time. Sometimes we'd set up lights inside, add a TV, and watch cartoons. Yes, it makes a total mess, but the cleanup is quick—and the memories? They'll last a long time.

Target shooting. Find ways to let them shoot airsoft guns, bow and arrows, and paintball guns. Safely, of course, and supervised by you. Some think I'm horrible for advocating any kind of shooting. They associate it with violence, and they don't allow their kids to play with toy guns. I hear you, but it's something that comes naturally with boys. A hunter instinct maybe. You can eliminate every toy gun out of the house, but if you have a boy, he'll make an imaginary pistol with his hand. Boys will shoot whether you let them touch a gun or not. If they're going to shoot, you might as well help them improve their aim.

Blast off. Build model rockets together and shoot them off. I'm talking about the type you load with an ignitable fuel "engine" off a launchpad. They're cheap, and kids love them. If you've got an open field around anywhere, this will give you and the kids hours of fun. After so many flights the rockets get a little too beat to fly anymore. We'd retire them to the bookshelves in the boys' room. As a dad, I saw them as trophies.

Games. Puzzles. Board games. Legos. Stuff you can do as a family—not the electronic "games for one." Let them use their imagination. Make up games. Kids can make a game out of anything. We made a game of throwing empty plastic milk cartons into the recycling bin—from increasingly greater distances. And hide-n-seek games are always fun. We played jail tag more hours in the kids' lifetime than I can imagine.

Get out of your chair. You're tired. You've worked hard. You don't feel like playing with the kids. Or maybe you're with friends and you'd rather sit with the adults. I get it. But get up anyway. Play with the kids. Chase them around the house or the yard. Tie on a cape, for Pete's sake. You may look silly to others—but I'll bet your wife will love you all the more for it. And the kids will squeal with delight, which is a lot more than the adults will do if you stay in that chair.

I could go on and on with things we did with our kids, but that isn't the point of this chapter. The point is simple. Your kids will be grown before you know it. Get creative. Spend time *together*, not just in the same room. There's a big difference.

I don't look back on the years we raised our kids with all kinds of regrets over missed opportunities. I totally enjoyed my kids, but I'd still give almost anything to have them small again—for one more day. And if I had that day, I wouldn't waste a second on the computer, the phone, the TV, or anything else. I'd be romping with them. Wrestling. Playing jail tag. If that day fell in the winter, we'd build a snow fort with at least one tunnel. And we'd be out there with flashlights at night—just like we used to do. If that day fell in the summer? We'd be in the lake, swimming or snorkeling. Playing alligator or jail tag again. We'd have a picnic in the little outboard at sunset and watch the stars come out.

Excuse me while I wipe the tears from my eyes. I mean seriously, I loved being a parent. You'll never regret investing your time, resources, and freedom in your spouse and your kids. *But watch the little things.* The little time and attention stealers.

⋆ ⋆ ⋆

Your kids will be grown before you know it. Get creative. Spend time *together*, not just in the same room. There's a big difference.

⋆ ⋆ ⋆

Even though I deliberately tried to make good choices as to spending time with my kids as they grew up, if I had a chance to do it again, I'd make even *better* ones. Because raising kids with my wife was *that* good. And it went so fast.

Did you ever watch the movie *Schindler's List*? Schindler was a German businessman during World War II. He operated a factory making much-needed munitions for the German war machine. The workers were Jews. And every Jew employed was a man or woman saved from the horrors of the Holocaust.

Eventually Schindler resorted to paying off officials to keep his workers—and to save them from certain death. Germany fell, and as the movie ends, Schindler was surrounded by grateful men and women—workers from his factory. People he saved.

But Schindler was haunted by regrets. He looked at his car with remorse. He remembered other little luxuries he had afforded himself that no longer held any meaning, realizing he could have used them to save more lives. To change the future.

It's a moving scene, and one that makes me think of what I'm trying to convey to you now.

Let me take one more swing at it. When your kids are grown and you look back at your years with them, you'll find no satisfaction in the time you spent selfishly. The real joy comes from remembering the time you invested in your wife and kids.

And *invested* is the right word. When you spend time with the kids like this, you'll impact them in countless ways. They'll be better balanced. More skilled socially. Have a healthier self-image. They'll have more love and respect for you, and that will make it just that more likely that they won't rebel. If you're living the Christian life for real, you'll be their hero. And chances are the kids are going to love God and want to serve him just like you hope they will.

God gives you three things. Time, resources, and the freedom to spend it however you want. Choose wisely.

Watch for Wobbles

I want you to get this. Want you to experience the wonder of marriage and parenting to the level God designed it to be. And in this last chapter, there's one more secret to get you there.

You've seen the circus entertainer routine where a guy balances a plate on a stick and gives it a spin, right? He keeps adding sticks and plates while running back and forth to give wobbling plates another spin. Eventually he has so many going—and so many plates losing momentum—that you're sure one of them will crash to the floor before he can get to it.

That's a picture of how life can be. We're balancing all sorts of responsibilities. Our spiritual life. Marriage. Job. Sometimes school. Parenting. Ministry or service. And as we get older, we tend to add things. Activities for the kids. Interests. Commitments. Friends. We can be like that entertainer—just trying to give each of these areas a little spin, a little attention, so we can get to the next responsibility before it crashes.

So where's the priority? Which plates do you focus on? Many may tell you to focus on the plate that's the most wobbly. It's the "squeaky wheel gets the oil" principle. In some cases that policy will serve you well; in others it will be disastrous.

Here's the priority as I understand it.

Plate 1: Your Relationship with God

Pretty obvious, but let this sink in. If you don't maintain this daily, every other plate will fall eventually. *Every single one.*

Remember what flight attendants say in their pre-takeoff safety spiel? "In the unlikely event that the cabin loses pressure, oxygen masks will drop down from the overhead compartment." They stress putting your own mask on before you try to help someone else—like small kids you may be traveling with. Why? Without a steady flow of oxygen you won't be able to help others for long.

The same principle applies to your personal walk with the Lord. If you don't maintain that, if you don't stay connected to him, you won't be able to help those you love. You'll be tempted to let that plate go a bit, to coast in your spiritual walk because of the demands of life. Don't do it. I've tried it—and it *doesn't* work.

Plate 2: Your Marriage

Not your ministry. Not your job. Not your kids. It's your marriage. Some will argue this point—especially if they're involved in ministry. Somehow they put ministry on the same plane as their relationship with God.

But your dedication to your marriage comes before ministry. *Before.* This is my opinion, but I think I can back it up scripturally.

Titus 1 and 1 Timothy 3 both list things that are prerequisites for a deacon or elder—a leader in the church. *The husband of one wife, managing his household well,* and things like that suggest that this man must be a good husband and dad. His marriage must be on a solid foundation—nothing shaky about it. It's a prerequisite. A qualifier. A given. If a man doesn't have a good marriage, he isn't eligible to serve at this level of ministry. Period.

I think that makes the point of your priority perfectly clear. Marriage before ministry—or you won't have a ministry. You're not even eligible. There are other passages I could take you to. First Peter 3:7 is one example: "Husbands, in the same way be considerate as you live with your wives, and treat them with respect as the weaker partner and as heirs with you of the gracious gift of life, so that nothing will hinder your prayers."

Serious stuff, right? Men, God makes it pretty clear that if your relationship with your wife isn't right, your relationship with him won't be right. If your relationship with him isn't right, you have no business ministering to others.

So if what I'm saying is true, if your marriage plate takes priority over ministry, how diligent do you need to be with that plate? Do you dare let it get wobbly? Let me ask it a different way. Do you want wobbly answers to prayer? Read 1 Peter 3:7 again. See what I mean?

You know your wife, so you'll be the best to detect if something isn't right. You'll see it in her eyes. Her attitude. Her perspective on things.

But knowing her now isn't enough. *She'll change.* Everybody does. Cheryl and I have gone through so many changes, and we're closer now than ever. We've changed in many good ways. That's the way it's *supposed* to be. Sanctification does a lot to change us—and our perspectives, dreams, desires. You'll both be changing. Keep up with her and stay close. As husbands, we can't afford to be overconfident. I've been married over thirty-three years. But I've only been in a thirty-three-year marriage for a short time. In that sense, I'm a newbie. Still learning. Things change. Keep up.

I'm thinking right now about a guy I've known for years. He actively served at his local church but got sloppy about his marriage. He controlled too much. Micromanaged. He didn't speak to his wife with enough love and was too slow making changes. And honestly, she did her fair share of demolition on their marriage as well.

Now they're divorced—with two sweet kids impacted for their entire lives. Tragic. The thing that really gets me is this. How did it get so bad? She said she doesn't love him and stopped loving him a long time ago. How did he not see that? How could he not tell in her eyes, her kiss, her enthusiasm to be with him? And if he saw it, how did he let that go so long without doing something about it?

He put other things ahead of her, no doubt. He didn't keep her plate spinning. When talk of divorce started, he tried taking the time to invest in their marriage and was willing to make changes or go to counseling, but she wasn't interested anymore. She didn't care. Wanted out.

His marriage plate crashed to the floor and shattered. He couldn't put it back on the stick and give it a spin. And how many other areas of his life fell apart as a result? Plenty. He resigned from his ministry duties. But the kids. The *kids*. Part of their world shattered, too. All the money in the world can't put their lives together again.

I'm not saying the woman was justified here. She was so, so wrong. She let things go as well. But he, as leader of the family, bears a heavy responsibility for how things turned out.

So don't wait until you see a wobble. Keep giving that marriage plate a spin whether it looks like it needs it or not. That's done in a lot of little ways—many of which we've talked about in previous chapters. Some people say marriage takes work. That's true, but when you get to a certain point I think *maintenance* is a better word for it. It's about actively protecting something that is or has the potential to be incredibly valuable.

Plate 3: Your Kids

Kids don't become part of your marriage plate. You don't switch out your plate for your wife and get one that says *family* on it. Your wife's plate is always her own.

Each of your kids gets their own plate. They fall in priority just after marriage, and just before your job/ministry plate.

Remember, your wife should come before the kids. Don't let that priority get reversed where the kids edge out your wife. And be sure your wife doesn't let the kids edge out *you*.

Plate 4: Your Job or Ministry

Most guys get this when it comes to a job. But the priorities can get a little fuzzy when they're in ministry.

If you're in ministry, remember your kids are still the higher priority. You want to impact other people for Christ. Show them a great, loving marriage, a strong family, and they'll see something they want. If your marriage, your family, is as messed up as theirs, you'll have nothing to offer. If you plan to encourage people to follow God's plan for love and marriage, your marriage had better be great. If your marriage isn't a great example of what God can do for couples committed to him, you're selling God short.

This is especially true with your own kids as they grow up. Unless they see your faith making a difference in your marriage, they'll leave home believing Christianity doesn't work, or it's not worth working at.

Never let the marriage plate wobble. Most couples start out well in marriage. Then a job takes priority. Or ministry. Or kids. They move on to other plates and neglect their marriage. Everything in life hinges on your keeping the marriage great. Don't wait for that plate to start wobbling before you give it attention.

When I used to scuba dive in Lake Geneva I'd tow a little float around so the spotters in the boat knew exactly where my buddy and I were. As I'd explore along the bottom I'd hear the motor start up, pull close, and cut occasionally. I'd know Cheryl, or whoever was in the boat, was right there.

One time I realized I hadn't heard the motor in a while. I signaled to my buddy and we decided to surface. We found Cheryl couldn't get the motor started and we'd drifted apart. It was scary. My buddy and I were sitting ducks in the water. We could have been killed by one of the many speedboats roaring by as we surfaced. I'd been doing my thing and expecting Cheryl to stay close to me. I totally changed my procedure after that to make sure *I* stayed close to her and the boat.

That's a little like marriage. Don't drift apart. Stay on guard—and make needed adjustments pronto. Don't expect your wife to do all the work. You need to work at it to stay close to her, too. This is part of your job as a man.

Concluding Thoughts

The introduction opened this book with an excerpt from a Levi's ad. In its own way, it was a call to manhood for a society that has grown complacent. Maybe the ad did some good—but that's probably just wishful thinking. But if God would grant me three wishes for you, here's what they'd be.

1. **That you'll be a hero.** That you'd do the right things and not quit—even when it's hard. That you'll love God with all your heart. That you'll accomplish the plans God has for you—with his help.

2. **That you'll have an excellent marriage.** It's so doable. Following

212   Super Husband, Super Dad

the principles in this book, and obviously in God's Book, will help you
move in the right direction.

3. That you'll be an excellent dad. And as a result, that your kids
grow to love God and follow him with all their heart.

With God's help, a watchful eye, and a lot of dedication, these three
things are exactly what you'll have. Regardless of where you are right
now or where you've been, with God's help you can make things better—and finish strong.

That's hero stuff, men. The cape is optional, but being a hero is not.

> Blessed are all who fear the LORD,
> who walk in obedience to him.
> You will eat the fruit of your labor;
> blessings and prosperity will be yours.
> Your wife will be like a fruitful vine
> within your house;
> your children will be like olive shoots
> around your table.
> Yes, this will be the blessing
> for the man who fears the LORD.
> —Psalm 128:1-4

One more thing, men. Do you mind if I talk to your wife for a
few minutes? I added a section to this book just for her. I just want to
remind her of a few quick things so she can help you be the hero she
really wants you to be. If you're okay with that, just pass the book to
her and ask her to read "A Word to the Wife."

★ ★ ★

A Word to the Wife

If you've read this book, or parts of it, maybe you've prayed that your man will make some of the changes I've urged him to make. You want him to be a hero as a man, a husband, and a dad. I want to encourage you and show you a few ways that you can help. I don't think most women realize how much they can influence their man—for good or for bad. First, something really foundational.

Love and Respect

Men need respect and women need love is a misunderstood cliché. Some years back an author tried to be helpful by summing up one of the differences between men and women with a little piece of insight. "Men need respect, and women need love." I never read the book, and I imagine the whole concept is explained really well. But many others have never read the book either…which leaves us with the cutesy saying—and a problem. The saying alone, without careful explanation, is a bit misleading.

Unless you get this, you're going to misunderstand your man, and you'll miss something in your marriage. So let's take a look at it.

Imagine this scenario. I am living in a time and in a country that punishes thieves severely. A man caught stealing has a hand chopped off. Ouch.

Now, let's say I've been caught stealing, and the authorities call in the guy with the big sword.

"Hold out a hand," the official orders, "or we'll take them both." He points to a wooden chop block with hack marks and bloodstains.

There is no way around this. I must hold out a hand—and fast— or lose them both. Now this official doesn't care *which* hand I hold out. He just wants to see one of them lying on the ground.

I'm right-handed. So which arm do I stretch out in front of the guy with the giant cleaver? *My left.* If I must make a choice and live with only one hand, I will choose to live with my right.

And so, back to our love and respect issue. Somewhere I suppose men were surveyed and asked, "If you could only have one, love or respect, which would you choose?"

It's really an unfair question. "Well, I'd really like both."

The man with the cleaver approaches. "You must choose only one."

"Well, if I can *only* pick one…"

Men can't choose love. Why? Because if a man is loved but not respected, it will make them feel like less of a man. Love without respect feels a lot more like pity.

"Gee, you really fall short of being a real man, so I can't respect you, but for some reason I just can't help loving you."

Thanks, but no thanks. A man needs to be respected by his wife. Otherwise he doesn't feel worthy of her love. He feels like a charity case.

So if a man was surveyed, and he had to pick one, love or respect, his manhood would prompt him to choose respect.

But he wouldn't be happy about it.

A man wants love, too. *That* is the truth. He needs love *and* respect. And the wise woman will work toward giving him both.

Hold on. What about Scripture? Women are instructed to respect their husbands.

> However, each one of you also must love his wife as he loves himself, and the wife must respect her husband (Ephesians 5:33).

Okay. But that certainly doesn't mean they aren't expected to love them. Love is a given. Expected of *every* Christian toward another

Christian. First Corinthians 13 backs that up, along with plenty of other scriptures.

Love and respect take deliberate effort on your part. Think about the way you treat your husband. The way you listen. The way you talk to him or about him. Are you showing him love and respect? Are you quick to criticize or to point out his flaws? Do you shoot down his ideas and input? When you confront him (even when he's clearly in the wrong), are you careful to do it like Abigail and Esther did in the Old Testament stories? Are you rationing out sex based on your needs or desires? There are lots of ways a wife can get a little relaxed showing her man love and respect. If you really want to do it right, ask him occasionally, "How can I show you more love and respect?" Men want to be truly loved *and* respected…and most would give their right hand to get it.

Going the Second Mile

In chapter 14 we covered a dozen ways men could help make their marriage stronger and keep it strong. Much of it will help you as well. But there are some things I want to say just to you.

Watch for and reward any steps in the right direction.

In this book your husband is being encouraged to be a better husband and dad. I'm leaning on him. Expecting him to get a chest. To man up. Here's what I need you to do: Watch for any little step in the right direction. You'll want to encourage it. Show him you noticed. Show him it matters. That you appreciate it. And show that appreciation in his love language if you want to make sure he gets the message.

If he makes some kind of attempt to improve and you don't seem to notice, or you notice but it doesn't seem like a big deal to you, he may give up and go back to old ways. You don't want that happening.

Work on your marriage daily.

Strive to find ways to show your man love, in his love language, daily. I know…you're busy and tired. But some things don't take a lot of time or energy. What would he appreciate?

Don't miss the little things. When you see his name come up on your cell phone, answer it like you're really glad to talk to him. When you see each other at home after work, hug him like he's the best part of your day. Tell him what you love about him regularly. Things you appreciate. How you're proud of him. This is really important.

Take some time to listen to him with your full attention. Sometimes a man needs to see that you care about what he's doing at work. What he's feeling about work. His worries. His fears. His excitement. He wants your approval as much as he wants it from the boss. Probably more.

Make your date great.

I've encouraged your husband to take you on regular dates. And here are some reminders to help you make the date great for both of you. And when both of you are enjoying the dates, the chances that your husband will keep initiating dates goes way up.

Do your part to make the date special. Anticipate it. You might leave a note for your husband in the car, or send a quick text during the day telling him how you can't wait for your date. That will make him look forward to it even more.

Wear something nice. When you were dating before you were married, you would have made an effort to do that. When you change clothes for your date, it somehow makes the whole night more special and more like a real date.

Keep things positive. Be careful not to criticize or put him down. My wife, Cheryl, and I don't usually talk about projects we need done around the house, either. The last thing you want on a date is to get your man thinking about all he has to get done instead of thinking about you. Make date conversations about good things. Talk. Listen. Dream.

Use that woman's intuition thing you have. Use that extra sensitivity for the sake of your marriage. Can you tell if he's had a bad day? Of course you can. So ask him about it in a nice way. A woman can encourage and strengthen a man like nobody else can.

Show some affection. Hold his hand. Take his arm as you walk. If he puts his arm around you, lean into him a little. And kiss him. Give him the good ones. Physically show you love him, and that you love being with him. A date should be an oasis. An escape, just for the two of you. And be thinking about having some intimacy with your husband afterward. He probably is. Okay, he *definitely* is. And in his mind, there's no better way to top off a date night with you. And that's a good thing—for both of you.

Keep growing spiritually and as a wife.

Ask God to change you, to help you be the woman, the wife you should be by the power of his Holy Spirit in your life. And get into the Word daily. As you truly live it out, you'll become more humble, quicker to forgive, and more aware of your shortcomings. This makes a huge difference.

First Peter 3:1-6 tells a woman how she is to live with a husband who isn't walking with the Lord. It talks about the power she has to influence her husband, to win him over by her behavior. It tells how a woman can do that without even speaking a word to her husband about it. It is about being beautiful inside—having a quiet, gentle spirit.

I can testify that God has used Cheryl in my life countless times to help me become the man I should be. She has loved me through my pride and selfishness to become a better man and follower of Christ. I don't think anything in my life could have influenced me more. That's part of the beauty of marriage.

Christian men can have moments or go through stages where they are not living out the Word, and you as women, by your spirit, by your behavior, are designed by God to help draw a man to the Lord. Whether your husband is a Christian or not, the Word should have such an effect on how you live as a wife that your husband will love you more and want to follow God more.

For example, Philippians 2:14 says, "Do everything without grumbling or arguing." Think about that. *Everything.* What an impact that can have on a husband. Living out what the Word says should have a profound effect on your marriage.

And if your husband isn't interested in church or doesn't want to go with you, take hope in 1 Peter 3:1-6. When you come home after church, give him all the love you can. A man would never hold a woman back from going to church if she came home ready to love him more instead of being tired and wrung-out. In fact, I think it might even make a man think about going to church with her—without being asked to do it. Gee, that would kind of fit with what 1 Peter 3:1-6 was pointing out.

Make sex a priority.

First Corinthians 7:5 warns us not to refrain from sexual relations with our spouse except by *mutual consent* and for the *purpose of prayer*. And the passage makes it clear it should be for a limited time to avoid temptation.

It doesn't recognize being tired or not being in the mood as valid reasons.

Sex is God's design. God's plan. This is part of God's will. This is something that can be tough, but we need to work at it. This command is just as much a part of the Bible as truths like *love your neighbor, trust in the Lord with all your heart, forgive others as God has forgiven you,* and *pray without ceasing.*

When you hold back on sex or ration it out, you are no longer driving down God's highway for marriage. You're off-roading somewhere down a well-traveled path. Many marriages go that route, but that doesn't make it the *best* route. Whenever you ignore God's plan you are choosing the second best. You are robbing your marriage of so many good things, so much strength that it could have.

Disagreements and arguments because of sex are one of the biggest areas of conflict between married couples. It doesn't have to be that way. Yes, for some men sex is primarily an urge. A need. Many men ignore their wives during the day but expect sex at night. That is wrong. Stupid.

But the cycle has to stop. Even if he doesn't work on his end to comply with Scripture, you still have a responsibility on your end. Your obedience to Scripture isn't dependant on whether or not your husband is worthy. Sometimes if a couple begins to have more sex, some of the other problem areas between them begin to straighten out. The importance of sex in marriage is staggering. When a man feels he isn't getting enough sex, he probably won't be treasuring his wife the way he should, either. It becomes a vicious cycle.

And some men are misjudged. Sex is more than an urge. It is their ultimate expression of love. This is the way God designed things. Remember the old saying? "The way to a man's heart is through his stomach." It simply isn't true for many, many men. But then you already knew that.

I was on faculty at a Christian writers conference and happened to be sitting at a cafeteria table with five or six ladies. The women were talking about sex, and specifically about frequency. They were complaining about how much their husbands "needed it." I felt invisible. They didn't seem to notice a man was sitting at their table.

One woman who was particularly resentful of her husband's sex drive said, "I give him enough sex."

It was the last straw for me. "Ladies," I said, smiling, "I'm sitting here listening to all this husband-bashing going on. Do you care to get a viewpoint from a man?"

They chuckled and invited me to share.

"Okay, you say you give him enough sex, but enough in whose opinion? Many men would love sex three times a day. So if you have sex with him twice a week because *you* think it's enough, you may be satisfied…but your husband is far from it. Don't you think he might resent that? And if he resents you deep down, how might that be affecting the way he treats you? How might that affect the quality of your marriage?"

The ladies weren't chuckling at this point.

I scanned their faces. "Let me ask you another question. How long do you think it would take to satisfy your man? I'm talking about a quickie here. How long would it take for you to bring him to a climax? Five minutes? Ten?"

The women laughed again. Little Mrs. I-give-him-enough spoke first. "It wouldn't even take me five minutes with him."

Other women chimed in and nodded.

"Okay," I said. "Now, tell me this. How long do the two of you argue about sex? When he wants it, and you don't—how long do those conversations last?"

The women went silent. The answer was pretty obvious. The argument lasted more than five minutes.

"And then after you're done arguing about it, how long afterward do you feel that tension between you?"

Their faces confirmed what I already knew. And I had the opportunity to remind them of how much sex can do for a man and for their marriage. "Instead of arguing about it, why not smile and satisfy your man? You'll get to sleep a lot sooner. You'll probably sleep *better*, and you'll be strengthening your marriage in the process. Your husband will go to sleep appreciating you instead of resenting you."

Sex is God's invention. Besides making children, it was designed to provide for us. To protect us. To draw a man and wife together in a physical and emotional bond. Why would we want to ration something like that?

Make it easy for your husband to take the lead.

Most Christian women would like to see their husband be more of a leader in the home—especially in a spiritual sense. Sometimes there are things a wife can do to make it easier for her husband to lead…and there are things she can inadvertently do that will hold him back. Here are a couple things to consider.

Leadership involves style. Be aware of this. I've seen men lead in all kinds of ways. Some are loud and bold, upfront men. Others aren't real vocal, but when they speak, the room quiets and people lean forward. Your husband won't likely share your leadership style. So look for little ways he's leading—and follow his lead. Don't push for him to lead in a certain way that may not be his style at all.

Encourage him to lead spiritually. Not by telling him to take the lead. Not by getting impatient and pushing. But by complimenting him when he does. Let's look at some ideas.

Church attendance. Make it easy for him to go to church. Don't get too concerned about what he's wearing, or that he's running late. Do all you can to make it a good day for your entire family. And at night

About the Author

Tim Shoemaker is the author of eleven books and speaks around the country to men and to parent groups about living the Christian life in a way that influences the next generation. Happily married since 1980, Tim has three grown sons and is active in church leadership. His books include *Code of Silence, Back Before Dark, Dangerous Devotions for Guys,* and *Smashed Tomatoes, Bottle Rockets...and Other Outdoor Devotionals You Can Do with Your Kids.*

To learn more about Tim Shoemaker, visit **www.harvesthousepublishers.com.**

To him, it looks like you don't think he knows how to drive. It can be annoying and belittling.

Sometimes a wife discourages a man from taking the lead without her realizing it. Sometimes you need to go with his decision on an issue, like disciplining the kids, or whatever, just to reinforce the fact that you see him as the head. If you question it too much or keep saying, "Well, I think we should…" you are not encouraging or reinforcing leadership. You may be undermining it.

Let me encourage you to go the second mile. You can do this. You have more power to impact your marriage for good than you think. Your husband may not deserve it, in your opinion. But God does. He's the one who laid out a plan for what a loving marriage should look like. So show your love to God by loving your husband. And you just might find your husband starts going the second mile for you.

You want your man to be a hero. To do the right things—even when it's hard, even when he doesn't feel like it. And I know you can help him. God designed you for it—put you in your husband's life to help him. I pray you'll help your husband be a hero as a man, husband, and dad. And in my book, that makes you a hero, too.

be sure your day at church hasn't sapped all your energy. If you're too tired to be with your kids or husband in a meaningful way, you won't be encouraging church attendance like you could otherwise.

His Bible. Let's say he takes his Bible to church. That's a good thing. He is making a statement by doing that. So tell him you like the way he brings his Bible, or the way he opens it during the sermon. Likely he'll bring it more often. And if you see him reading his Bible during the week, walk right over and put your arms around him. Let him know how much you love seeing him in the Word.

His singing. If he sings during your church worship time, lean over and whisper that you love to hear him sing to God.

His opinion. Ask his opinion more when it comes to spiritual things. Don't always be so quick to tell him what Beth Moore said in the latest Bible study series. Instead, ask your husband about spiritual questions you have. Treat him like he is the leader. You might ask him something like, "I need some of your wisdom here…" and give him time to process it. Maybe the two of you are going on a date in a couple days. Give him some advance time to think about the question you have. "Hey, on our date Friday, I want to ask you about…"

Don't compete with church attendance. You want your husband to lead spiritually. You want him to be a good dad. But when you sign the kids up for Sunday sports you put those two goals in direct opposition to each other. In our culture, a man who doesn't attend his kids' sporting events is looked at as being kind of a deadbeat dad. So given a choice, a man will probably go to the game.

In general, practice letting him lead more in your marriage. As a wife and mom, you make a ton of decisions. When you're with the kids, you're in charge and you're playing the lead role. Remember to give that over to your husband when he's around.

A woman can be so used to giving the kids directions, she does that to her husband, too. Like when he's driving.

Do you know how fast you're going? He can read a speedometer.

Do you see that light just turned yellow? Yes, he knows his colors.

Aren't you going to turn here? There's more than one way to get someplace.